Mrs Boswell's Slice of BREAD

Me: the author

Mrs Boswell's Slice of BREAD

Carla Lane

and William Corlett

BBC Books

PICTURE CREDITS

Barnaby's Picture Library, pages 14 (Aca-press München/Armez) and 36 (Nick Scott);
Camera Press, page 86; John Mills Photography, page 9. The remaining photographs are
BBC copyright.
Front cover: the photograph of 'Mrs Boswell' was taken by Alistair Morrison, by courtesy of
Jean Boht.

Illustrator Jane Cradock-Watson

Published by BBC Books
A division of BBC Enterprises Ltd
Woodlands, 80 Wood Lane, London W12 0TT

First published 1989

ISBN 0 563 20829 5

Designed by Grahame Dudley Associates

Set in 11 on 13 pt Garamond by Ace Filmsetting Ltd,
Frome, Somerset
Cover printed by Fletchers Ltd, Norwich, Norfolk
Printed and bound in Great Britain by Richard Clay Ltd,
Bungay, Suffolk

Contents

Dedication

I DEDICATE THIS book to my family. Firstly, to our Aveline, my only daughter, recently taken from us and married to a Proddy vicar, may the good Lord bless and preserve us all in our time of need. (A Proddy vicar? As if I haven't brought her up a Christian all her life.) And then to my four sons, Joey, Adrian, Jack and Billy; also to my father who is still with us and eating for victory; and finally, if I must, to my husband, Freddie Boswell, the root of all my suffering and the reason for there being a book here in the first place. If he'd stayed put where he belonged and endeavoured to love, honour and obey – to say nothing of passing on a few of his worldly goods – instead of going off with a great, over-developed TART, we'd none of us have had to spend every waking minute over-exerting our creative faculties to provide ourselves with the living he never gave us.

Nellie Boswell

Chapter One

About Bonking

No, IT ISN'T going to be that sort of book and this will be the only time I'll use that word. But this chapter was originally called *Introduction* and I can never believe that anyone bothers with chapters like that. So, if I have to use a word like *bonking* to get attention, I'll just go out and do it.

Besides, in a way, the whole of this book will be about that over-rated pastime. A woman's life is one long wrestle from beginning to end. And, speaking as the mother of one daughter and four sons, it's not just the women who're in danger now. The men don't stand a chance either. I was watching the girls in town yesterday, walking around with their skirts up to their pierced ears, and their chests doing the highland fling beneath their jumpers. When I was a girl, your chest wasn't allowed to create a disturbance, it was hoisted up beneath your chin in mortal silence. And so it should be. In fact, I could as easily have called this chapter *Marauding Breasts* – for that's another of life's dangerous little ironies – men's incessant fascination with the mammary glands. Because that's all they are; a functional part of the female anatomy; like little toes or nostrils. You don't find grown men going potty over a woman's nostrils. Well, not respectable men. But my husband had only got to clap eyes on Lillian Whittacker – known to all the world as Lilo Lil, and I don't think I need to explain why – and he was off like a cat off a hot plate. And why? What was it that Miss Whittacker had that was so special? Nothing! Nothing except a chest that lives a life of its own. If I had grown into a 'Z' cup, none of the following pages would have been written.

But if I am to tell the story of my life, such as it is, then I'm leaping ahead. That's what bitterness can do to you. It gets inside you, like yeast in bread, and makes you swell up until you think you'll explode. I WILL NOT SPEAK ABOUT THAT TART UNTIL THE TIME IS RIGHT, AND WHEN I DO, I WILL TELL ALL.

I can't claim to have had a very adventurous life. I'm now living in the house where I was born, and my mother before me, No 30 Kelsall Street. I only ever moved once

Liverpool - where it all happens.

and that was when I married Freddie Boswell. With him I took up residence at No 28 Kelsall Street, the house next door. For reasons of duty and economy which I'll go into later, the family had to move back here when Freddie went off with that TART and Grandad moved into No 28. We each pay identical rent and claim it back from the DHSS. In this way, we are able to benefit a little from the Welfare State into which we would willingly plough our honest earnings if we could only get jobs with which to earn the earnings. However, to continue with my own saga – which may not be *Gone With The Wind* but has had its moments and a scarlet woman who makes all others fade into a hint of pink (and please note, Vivien Leigh didn't need a big chest to succeed) – this kitchen, in which I am now sitting writing these words, has been my home and work place for as many years as I can remember. Of course, the passage of time has brought many alterations. Going on the family motto that 'The Best Things In Life Are Expensive', we have made certain improvements that have transformed what would otherwise have been an ordinary terrace residence into a shrine to the technological and gastronomical age. A microwave oven, a six-slice toaster and a fully automatic washing machine may not be every maiden's dream, but they certainly oil the wheels for a woman who spends nine-tenths of her life skateboarding between the cupboards and cooker for the good of her family.

Even so I must admit that sometimes I look round and I think – How did it happen to me? How did Nellie Duvall (that was me), who could turn a few heads in her time down at the clubs in her slinky red velvet and black feather boa, end up as Nellie Boswell, having a deeply meaningful relationship with an ironing board and a sink disposal unit which, in common with most of the men in her life, chews up the scraps and spits them straight in her face instead of swallowing them like all self-respecting units are supposed to do. How *did* it happen?

Five pregnancies, that's how. Five times shoving and heaving and sweating. Five healthy babies and thirty years of motherhood. I sometimes think I'll end up with four, fifty-year-old teenagers, skating up the hall, and one married daughter going forth and multiplying – thus tipping the population scales in favour of the Proddies. But then I ask myself, how do Protestants ever manage to make babies in the first place? They're too boring to reach an orgasm. They'd fall asleep before the earth had a chance to move! I'm sure their God must have turned off the sound and only be watching the pictures. Have you heard the voice the vicars use when they speak to him. Poor man! What did he do to them that they have to bore him like that? Listening to a Proddy vicar saying prayers is like an amateur production of *The Desert Song* – no passion from The Red Shadow and precious little tune. I should know, I've got one for a son-in-law; a Proddy vicar I mean – not a Red Shadow. Besides which, I'm not at all sure that God speaks English anyway. I mean he may have made us all in his image but that doesn't mean to say he necessarily sounds like us. I must speak to Father Dooley about this. Father Dooley is our priest and confessor and when he's not backing the horses or drinking gin, he has a lot to say about the Latin mass. Latin was a universal language; the Holy Father could travel to any country and address God straight off. But now that they've dropped the Latin mass, the present Pope, God bless him, who is always off on some Papal Package Tour, must have that many phrase books they'll need a special Popemobile to carry them.

However, what the Holy Father does or says really has very little to do with this book – though we did have a family trip to Rome and I will be including our album of the event later on.

It may seem surprising to you that a woman like me should turn to writing. But then most women writers are like me: stuck in a kitchen when they're not running to do the bidding of their lord and master; a slave to their offspring; cook, cleaner, counsellor, psychiatrist, doctor, vet . . . Ask Fay Weldon or Shirley Conran or that woman who wrote *The Valley Of The Dolls*, our Jack's favourite book (apart from the antique guide, which he uses to check out how he makes so many useless deals). They'll all tell you the same thing. They got fed up mashing potatoes and watching the world passing them by. So I thought – if they can do it, why can't I? I must also admit that Celia Higgins, my friend and neighbour, encouraged me. She has had a book published and she still gets royalties from it. Well, if Celia can do it . . . I mean, her life is as tangled as a plate of spaghetti. Men, of course. Too many of them and never the right one. So, if you think about it, why not me? Nellie Boswell, Booker Prize Winner.

This book will be my personal contribution to the family pot. So, whoever you are reading this, please don't lend it to your friends – tell them to go out and buy their own copy. It may not make you feel generous, but it'll make a Scouse family very happy and you can take comfort from that.

There are two books that have inspired me in a way and one newspaper.

The books are: *Mrs Beeton's Book of Household Management* and *The Country Diary of an Edwardian Lady*.

The newspaper, you may be surprised to know, is the *News of the World*.

I would like to reassure you that we do not have the *News of the World* delivered to this house but it sometimes manages to infiltrate its way into our living-room. Like an illegal immigrant, it's smuggled in under the jacket of one or other of the inhabitants – and it's significant that since our Jack's been exiled in America, it hasn't been much in evidence. I would never read it myself and I'd prefer the others not to, but I have glanced at it, when throwing it away wrapped in kitchen towel – you can't trust the dustmen round here, they'd go through the contents of a hoover bag looking for gold dust. So how does this disgusting rag come to be an inspiration to me? It has given me the courage to tell all, about a certain person who shall be nameless at the moment but who is a TART and who won't know what's hit her when I get to her, the pen being even mightier than the gob. Or in this case the word processor, for which I am indebted to my eldest son, Joey, and to the DHSS Youth Opportunities Scheme which apparently doesn't exist any more, but which Joey managed to get back-dated. (He could get your birth certificate back-dated, our Joey.)

The family. Husband at home for once.

Mrs Beeton's I got off my Grandma, who got it off a man whose wife worked for a family in Gateacre. I've never used it as a cookbook, of course – anyone who did would be dead by now either from salmonella poisoning or cardiac arrest – but I like to think it has a bit of class and is obviously written by a woman who spent most of her life looking at the inside of a mixing bowl, so there's a kindred spirit there.

The Country Diary I got for Christmas one year from our Jack and Adrian. They bought it at an auction, believing it to be a first edition. Which it probably is, in its way. It's pretty to look at, but it's a pity it has *Property of Liverpool Public Library* stamped on every other page. I can't say I feel I have much in common with the author. Edwardian ladies would appear to have had a lot of time on their hands.

I hope that this book will become required reading for every poor girl about to set up home with a fella – and for some poor fellas about to set up home with a fella, the way things are going. I thank God on my knees constantly that it doesn't seem to be the direction my Adrian is heading in after all – though only time will tell. I still don't think he's worked out what to do with a woman and we do already have one relative who is gay, so nothing is certain. Not that I have anything against gays, as long as they're not my sons.

It's a funny thing, you know. After my husband left home for the first time to set up his den of adultery with that TART, I used to lie in bed at night, in the dark room, with only my thoughts for company. I would wonder how the children would turn out. I had visions of failing to guide them properly. I was convinced that as there was no dad in the house I'd end up with a prostitute, a gangster, a kleptomaniac, an alcoholic and a poof. So far, we seem to have escaped and if that isn't a living proof of the power of prayer, I don't know what is.

So the following pages will be about what I really know: my family. And believe me, if you sit at the end of the dinner table and keep your ears stretched there isn't anything any of them gets up to that I haven't a pretty clear picture of. With one daughter, four sons, one geriatric, a mongrel dog and an errant husband, I think I'm well suited to understand the mysteries of life.

But because I want this to be a useful book as well – otherwise it's once read and onto the shelf until someone comes round collecting, usually for a Proddy vicarage garden party – I will include some of my special recipes and other useful household tips. A sort of Scouse Katie Boyle really:

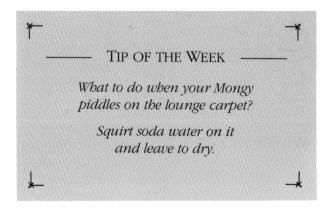

—— TIP OF THE WEEK ——

*What to do when your Mongy
piddles on the lounge carpet?*

*Squirt soda water on it
and leave to dry.*

(It took me months to convince Billy that Katie didn't mean drowning the dog in Schweppes.)

There will be snaps from our family album; art work and poetry from Adrian; notes on fashion; and all the flotsam and jetsam of family life.

And as for the 'bonking' with which I started this chapter, it seems such an insignificant little word to describe something that makes or breaks our lives. But I suppose everything is about it really. So, inevitably there will be a lot of it in this book. I can't avoid it because that's where all the trouble starts. With bonking, or as I prefer to call it, hanky-panky.

We were put into this world, I sometimes think, by hanky-panky, for hanky-panky and, if we're not very careful, it'll be hanky-panky that'll carry some of us out of it.

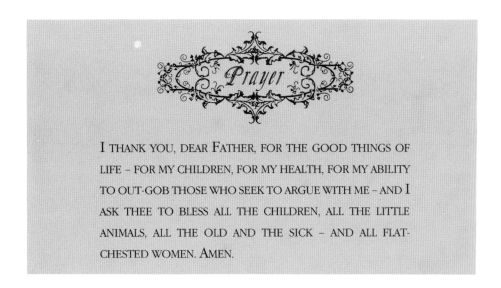

Prayer

I THANK YOU, DEAR FATHER, FOR THE GOOD THINGS OF LIFE – FOR MY CHILDREN, FOR MY HEALTH, FOR MY ABILITY TO OUT-GOB THOSE WHO SEEK TO ARGUE WITH ME – AND I ASK THEE TO BLESS ALL THE CHILDREN, ALL THE LITTLE ANIMALS, ALL THE OLD AND THE SICK – AND ALL FLAT-CHESTED WOMEN. AMEN.

Chapter Two

Early Days

I CAN'T PRETEND that we knew at the time that we were living through the 'swinging sixties': espresso coffee and the Beatles; 'would you let your daughter go out with Mick Jagger?' and the Profumo affair. It was as though the whole of life was happening somewhere else – just down the road and round the corner. Nothing seemed to swing in Kelsall Street. But they weren't bad times all the same. I've looked at Aveline sometimes and wondered if she was having the carefree life that we had. Or does it only seem like that now? Does the past always seem a bit brighter, more coloured, lighter and easier than the present?

Well that's how I remember it anyway. Tottering down Lime Street on stiletto heels with my hair in a beehive. Straight into the arms of Freddie Boswell. He wasn't the first nor was he the most pressing. I'd had other offers of matrimony. I could now be living in the outback of Australia if I'd taken up one. Or then there was Billy Bartington; he wanted to marry me and he is now an interior designer for the stars of *Dallas*. I could even now be riding round in an extended limousine when I wasn't in having my face re-arranged. But no; I fell for tatty face and his fancy talk – a lad with a shock of hair like a Brillo pad and clothes that came from the back room of an Oxfam shop (that's where the stuff even the Third World rejects is stored). And yet, in a way, looking back, he was the first real boyfriend I had. All the others were make-believe. I was a young girl then, with dreams, the Belle of the Grafton, that was me. And he? He used to buy me Jacqmar head scarves and real silk stockings. The others didn't get a look in.

Me in the early days

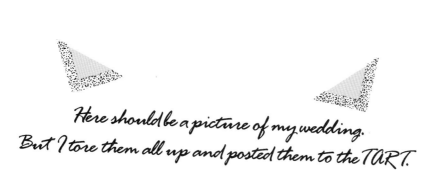

*Here should be a picture of my wedding.
But I tore them all up and posted them to the TART.*

We got married in St Jude's, the Catholic church that's dedicated to the saint for hopeless causes. The groom was waiting for me at the altar looking like a burst bolster, with his trousers held up with string. I knew he was up to no good when I saw him trying to persuade the priest to sell the chalice off the altar. But there we were for all that – man and wife. Mr and Mrs Freddie Boswell, No 28 Kelsall Street.

How many women realise on their wedding night that the road can only go downhill from now on? Most, I dare say. And yet in those days we were so hell bent on getting married. And I doubt things are all that different now, if Aveline is anything to go by. While I was dreaming of all the glamour of a top model for her, d'you know what she was yearning for? 'A normal life' – whatever that's supposed to be – with 'a little white pram on the garden lawn' – and a great big oaf in the back room waiting to be fed, if I know anything, and if he's not already off out up to hanky-panky with God knows who; except I did know, more's the pity.

My man hadn't the nous to keep it to himself. That's the trouble with romantics, they have to splash all their feelings out over everything and everybody. But then so it's always been. 'Days of adrenalin and hormones' according to Grandad, who, in his time, led my mother a merry dance with a woman called Edie Matheson. I ask you! Grandad! The most he ravishes now is a custard slice or a danish pastry. But there's something about the way he shovels in the food that suggests that given half-a-chance he'd be out there, up to no good, still. So I don't know why I thought things were going to be different for me. And, in a way, I could have stood it all: I could have borne the disappointments and the brief honeymoon before the hard work set in – if only she hadn't come along and torn it all apart. Lilo Lil, with her rapacious bosom. I never stood a chance, not really. I had lace on my knickers, she had warning lights on hers.

Not that we didn't have good times, Freddie and me. There was a lot of hanky-panky to begin with, of course there was, and I'm not saying I didn't enjoy it. He was a man, my Freddie – but not one I was going to share; not with anyone, let alone her. And anyway, then our Joey was born. There's nothing like a new baby to quench the

Jack, Aveline, Billy, Joey and Adrian – with me in the middle.

flames and put a blight on your nights of unbridled passion.

When I had Joey in the hospital, Freddie actually arrived; not quite in time, but you can't ask for the moon. I have to admit I was surprised when I saw him walking through the door. Does that mean I already had my doubts? No, I don't think so. I was just hedging my bets. But there he was – multicoloured like a rainbow, pissed out of his skull. He sat for twenty minutes at the next bed gazing at the wrong baby. Well, of course it's a nervous time for a man – particularly with the first. So I had to be charitable.

I didn't know how lucky I was that he was there at all. It turned out to be the first and last time I'd see him anywhere near my bed of labour.

When our Jack was born, he was playing darts in Blackpool. When our Adrian was born he was marching through the City protesting because they were pulling the Blue Bell pub down. With our Aveline he did turn up – but the following morning and carrying a book of boys' names. By the time our Billy was born of course, he was running bare-foot through Sefton Park with the one and only Lilo Lil.

Mind, he was in work then down on the docks and we didn't go short. I use the word 'work' loosely, you'll understand. When he was on nights, his mates used to scoop him up off the dock road and pour him on board. He'd book himself into a first class cabin, set the alarm for five minutes before the boss came in in the morning, get up, collect his tins of ham and his danger money, bribe the gate policeman and come home in time to watch racing on television. It put me off tinned ham for ever.

Our children followed in quick succession. We were going for the dozen – that's what he wanted. On one occasion, when I told him I was pregnant, he said, 'Never mind – you'll get better soon!'

It was his way, of course, his way of not letting people know what he was feeling. He does it now. He can still . . . hide . . . even from me. He was glad really. Glad I was pregnant.

Well, it was all right for him, wasn't it? He didn't have to carry them, did he? He didn't have to go round wearing smocks and taking cod liver oil, he didn't have to queue at the Maternity with his water specimen in an HP sauce bottle. He didn't have to lie there while the entire medical profession poked and peered about in his most secret places. All he had to do was 'nothing'. The name Freddie Boswell will go down in history as the major contributor to the art of NOTHING.

No, to be fair, not just Freddie – all men. I can't think what contribution they make to this life. Apart from the obvious one. Without Freddie I wouldn't have got my children and I'd be the poorer for that. But, forgive me Father for questioning, why didn't you make us like the flowers? It'd have been so simple. All we'd have to do was go out on a windy day and we'd be pollinated – it would save all that nonsense, all that fuss and fume.

So there we are, there wasn't much to tell. It seems as though I was only Nellie Duvall for a minute while no one was looking and I've been Nellie Boswell ever since.

But Father Dooley was right when he told me that God's work is like the Grand National – you should never bet on the Favourite for fear a Rank Outsider might just come over the sticks and finish first.

I've got a family – a united family and this is their story.

Prayer

I THANK YOU, DEAR FATHER, FOR ALL MY CHILDREN AND THE JOY THEY BRING ME WHEN THEY'RE NOT WORRYING ME HALF TO DEATH OR DRIVING ME INTO AN EVEN EARLIER GRAVE WITH THEIR SELF-OBSESSIONS. PLEASE LET JOEY CONTINUE TO DO WHATEVER IT IS THAT HE DOES, AS SUCCESSFULLY AS HE APPEARS TO HAVE DONE IT SO FAR. LET JACK COME HOME SAFELY FROM AMERICA WITHOUT HAVING CAUGHT AIDS. LET AVELINE MANAGE TO PUT UP WITH HER PRODDY VICAR AND HAVE CHILDREN AND NOT LOSE HER FIGURE WITH THE POST NATAL. LET ADRIAN MANAGE TO BE BOTH ARTISTIC AND VIRILE. AND, DEAR FATHER, IF IT ISN'T TOO MUCH TO ASK, LET BILLY, OUR YOUNGEST, LEARN NOT TO CHARGE AT LIFE LIKE A BULL AT A COW. AMEN.

Chapter Three

Joey (1): The Scourge of the DHSS

'GREETINGS!'

That, it is said, was the first word that our first-born ever uttered. It may seem unlikely and I can't vouch for it myself, because it was Freddie who claims he heard it when he came home one night from a darts match with the entire team. They had me making sandwiches in the kitchen while they stood round the cot singing unsuitable lullabies in doubtful harmony and at a volume that would have woken the dead on the Isle of Man. Eventually, Mrs Bradley at No 27 sent over her eldest, Stan, to say that if they didn't shut their gobs she'd have the police on them for assault and battery. Not wanting to digress too much, but it was her Stan who ended up inside a few years later for absconding with the takings of a milk round. The Bradleys were always too stuck up for their own comfort.

Anyway, on the particular night in question, a bit of hush having been achieved by the threats from No 27, allowed the baby the luxury of a bit of peace in which to drop off to sleep – which he'd been no doubt longing to do since the darts team so rudely barged into his nursery. (With only one baby there used to be room for a nursery. That was soon to change. And now of course, the house is not unlike a youth hostel – you never know who might be passing through. Though, unlike a youth hostel, there isn't any sharing out of the household chores!)

Our Joey was a perfect child from the moment he drew breath. He never cried at an inconvenient moment and he took to my milk in a way that none of the others did and with a suck on him like an industrial hoover. Left to his own devices I found he'd drop off to sleep quite happily. But Freddie was all for rocking him and nursing him. It's a wonder the boy didn't end up going to sea; the whole of his infancy was spent going through the motions of a force ten storm. His father just couldn't leave him alone. So, of course, when he came running into the kitchen that night I took very little notice.

'Nellie! Nellie!' he shouted, all breathless and glazed with ale (have you ever noticed how drink makes men's faces shiny?) 'He spoke! Joey! He spoke.'

'Well, he was going to sooner or later,' I told him. 'What did he say?' I knew it wouldn't be 'Mum': because Joey has never been predictable. It's not his style.

'Greetings!' Freddie spluttered pinkly. 'He just said "Greetings"!'

I must admit it seemed original. Personally I think he was probably just belching. But, as I say, Joey has always had a way of surprising people so I've never been quite sure.

It can't be easy being the eldest, and certainly not in our family, with a permanent absentee father. But Joey very soon established himself as the leader of the pack, my right hand – in every way the head of the family. I hope it hasn't been too hard on him over the years, but I know in my heart it has. He's never been able to have a life of his own. He's always put the family first.

That's Joey's philosophy.

How would I describe him? Say an alien arrived from another planet and wanted to be shown a perfect specimen of an earth creature, I don't think we could do any better than to roll out Joey as exhibit 'A'.

Celia Higgins took one look at him when she arrived in the street and declared him 'Gorgeous'. Mind she's predatory and old enough to be his mother. Well, almost. But then all the girls fancy Joey – with the possible exception of our Billy's Julie. But then she has a built-in resistance to anything with the surname Boswell.

Joey. The word 'cool' was coined specially for him. The concept of 'style' came about to accommodate him. Kindness and strength and enough charm to flood the Mersey: that's Joey Boswell.

It was natural that he should step into the Managing Director's seat and take over the running of the family business. Because that's what we've got: a thriving business. I wasn't going to have my family go under; we weren't going to be a statistic on the 9 O'Clock News. After Freddie walked out – well, you feel terrible when something like that happens. Particularly when I knew where he'd gone. I felt as though she was better than me. I felt all wrong. I wanted to crawl away into a corner and disappear. But I couldn't, could I? There were seven hungry mouths to fill; like feeding time at the seals' enclosure. All of them sitting there, honking and clapping their flippers: five kids, one grandad and an over-sexed mongrel dog. So I had to do something and I did the only thing I could.

My mother left me a tureen, shaped like a cockerel sitting on a nest. I put it in the middle of the table, lifted its lid and recited the parable of the talents. You know the one – where a certain man had three servants, and to one he gave five talents and to the second two talents and to the third one talent . . .

'The Family Pot' by Adrian Boswell, artist

'Well,' I said to them, 'I'm not sure what your talents may be – except for Adrian, of course (Adrian was at that time in real work – as you will discover later. You will also discover that being in real work brings in a very poor dividend) – but from now on, you've all got to get out there and use whatever talents the good Lord gave you to fill this pot so that we, as a family, may survive and prosper. Amen.' I excluded Grandad and Mongy, the dog, from this – though I would like to say that once in a while Mongy has brought back some very good meat and, on' one occasion a whole Stilton. As I didn't know where he had got it from, I couldn't return it and besides I don't think an animal can be expected to live by the same moral standards as us mortals. They're wild creatures, aren't they? They live by the law of the jungle. And in their defence, should they need any, the animals of the wild do not wage wars, lie, cheat or sin. They are in every way our superiors and it's about time mankind woke up to that fact.

'So,' I said to them, 'it's no use sitting waiting for our ship to come in – because ships don't come in to Liverpool any more.'

They were prophetic words. They've turned the Docks into a tourist attraction now, haven't they? We can stare at the beautiful buildings which we once took for granted and if we save up for a week we can have a cup of tea in one of the warehouses and crack Scouse jokes for the trippers, who'll ask to take our photographs and whether we're related to Cilla Black. 'Surprise! Surprise!' we can say with a merry wave, but meanwhile the body has to be fed.

Joey – the cool version

   I instilled in them the fact that it's a bad world out there. That they're only really safe in this house. 'We must go out there and beat them at their own game,' I said, but I added that they shouldn't do anything illegal or that could bring shame on the family. (I've always dreaded that what happened to the Bradleys could happen to us. They had a piece in the evening paper three nights in a row.) 'If we can't walk tall and proud, we won't be a united family,' I told them.

   And, of course, being Catholics we also have the benefit of the confessional. How the other side manage is a mystery to me. It must be like a house without an automatic washing machine with a double action spin dryer. I mean, you can hand wash –

Joey (1)

but it's a hard job to shift some of the darker stains, and it takes forever to get things really dry in this climate. That must be why the Proddies are always half damp.

Joey went straight down to the DHSS the following morning. He made the acquaintance of one of the young ladies there, who no doubt fell under his charms, though she must have been sex starved anyway, because later she was to have a brief spin on the sexual roundabout with a distant and doubtful cousin of the family, known for obvious reasons as Shifty. In my opinion any woman who fell for him would have as readily fallen for a blue-arsed baboon. But then all women are fools at some time in their lives and Celia Higgins assures me that even Shifty has something to recommend him.

So, nice and helpful she was, this girl at the DHSS. Name of Martina (Joey says you should always get the name of the secretary or the woman behind the counter). She gave him a book entitled *Are You Getting Enough?* which our Jack grabbed hold of for all the wrong reasons and soon put down when he discovered that it was a list of the benefits and allowances that we should all be aware of as our due, if we are to fulfil our obligations as members of a democratic society. It would be a terrible crime if the people we vote into the high office of government were making all these rules and regulations and none of us were taking advantage of them. That would be ungracious, I think, if not downright rude.

Under Joey's guidance we set about righting these discrepancies at once – and a lot of aggravation it caused us along the way but we didn't complain; we saw it as our duty as decent citizens.

For a start, we had to move here and Grandad had to move next door. Thus were the two households able to charge each other rent and the unemployed members of both houses were able to claim the rent back from the state. You see what I mean? That money was due to us and we'd done nothing about it. Joey endeavoured to have the claims back-dated, but this in the end proved unfruitful. Never mind. At least we asked – as every conscientious citizen should do.

Mongy – guarding the house and family

Family Saying

SOME YOU WIN.
SOME YOU HAVE TO POSTPONE.
KEEP ASKING.
YOU CAN'T FILL A BUCKET WITHOUT TAKING IT
TO THE TAP.

Since then Joey has managed to help the state to help us in innumerable different ways – some of which I'm not too sure about myself.

We claim an allowance for Mongy – as a guard dog. Which saves the state having to fork out every time the house would be emptied without him here. And don't think I'm being dramatic – the people round here would steal the pennies off a dead man's eyes.

We claim for a hearing aid for Grandad – in case his deafness gets any worse. Which, thank God, at the moment it doesn't seem to be doing. In fact there are times when I think he hears every word that is said in our kitchen even though he lives next door – either that or he's got second sight. But he's an old man – 75 – veteran of two world wars, fighting for his country. His hearing could go at any minute; no use then trying to get money towards a hearing aid. You know how slow government departments can be. We'd be claiming his death allowance before he ever heard again – which would be tragic. There's nothing Grandad likes better than a good chat.

Rose, the canary –
guarding Grandad

We also claim laundry allowance for Grandad's incontinence. Again this is, thank God, so far only a precaution – but once the water works go it's going to be a full-time job. Grandad has three bedrooms in that house. And many's the time he goes to bed in one room, gets up in the night to relieve himself, forgets which bed he was in, slips between a second pair of sheets and is off out of them into a third bed before the dawn has broken over the river's bank. Three lots of sheets in one night. We ought to have the allowance reviewed. We did claim for a guard dog for Grandad as well – feeling that Mongy's work was cut out looking after us. He bought a canary instead – which I daresay might alert him to an alien presence in the house if it were to whistle very loudly and flap its wings against the little mirror with the bell on it at the same time. The canary, incidentally, is called 'Rose' – which indicates the human face of caring.

Obviously all large bills go to the DHSS for their consideration: the electricity – they must think we're paying for Blackpool illuminations; British Telecom – a particularly grey area. How can we run up the bills they say we do? Where is the proof? Every time I telephone them I speak to a different recorded voice – are there no human beings left? When one of these recorded voices once actually answered me back, I discovered that they *are* humans . . . of a sort: British-Telecom-Humans – the kind with no heart, no humour and no hope.

Me with phone

> ——— HELPFUL TIP ———
> *Want to be in constant touch with a busy working family? Obtain some cordless 'phones. The new models will slip easily into a handbag or the pocket of a leather jacket and you can then call up your loved ones wherever you or they may be. Many's the time I've received a piece of vital information at the check-out of Tescos or at a matinée at the Odeon. They are also invaluable for a young girl out in the evil streets. One hint of a mugger, rapist or hijacker and out comes the cordless from the back pocket or the shoulder bag and it's straight through to the police with a quick 999.*

But they're all local calls. I've tried reaching Jack in Los Angeles more than once – without any success. So don't tell me a few local calls can add up to the zillions BT try to charge us every quarter. 'Private enterprise?' I said to the recorded voice. 'You lot must have solid gold furniture off our account alone. You must have taken figures out of a hat. Well, I'm not paying it!' and I slammed down the offending instrument or rather I pressed 'Clear' – as I was speaking on the cordless at the time, having opened the bill on my way to see Father Dooley for my absolution.

Joey leaves no stone unturned in his pursuance of the family's rights and dues. He parks his Jaguar within walking distance of that office and is in there on the dot of opening time every day that the Lord gives us.

In closing this chapter I thought I should ask Joey to speak for himself. What, I asked him, is the technique you use when visiting the DHSS Office. Here is the example he offered of the way the meeting could go.

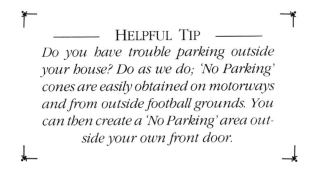

——— HELPFUL TIP ———
*Do you have trouble parking outside
your house? Do as we do; 'No Parking'
cones are easily obtained on motorways
and from outside football grounds. You
can then create a 'No Parking' area outside your own front door.*

Imagine, if you will, Martina the DHSS girl sitting behind her bullet-proof glass, her hair combed neatly and her hand poised above a stack of forms. Joey enters, bringing with him a warm whiff of a life beyond her narrow world. A freer life, with a wide horizon and HOPE writ large on the hills. A better life – working all day with biros and forms must blur your vision. You can't help feeling sorry for the girl, really.

'Greetings!' he begins.

Martina looks up.

Joey smiles. The sun comes out. His leather jacket gleams. His gold watch flashes at his wrist as he glances at it – our Joey has never got time to waste.

'Yes, Mr Boswell?' the iron maiden of the Social Services says, managing to speak without appearing to move her lips.

Joey has got her attention. Now he goes in:

'My aged grandad, whose little legs are like pipe cleaners and can no longer support him, and whose eyes are on a dimmer switch, whose heart beats faintly and whose frail hands can hardly lift a knife and fork would like . . .'

Lady Macbeth bridles and interrupts:

'I saw him sitting outside his house the other day. He had a tray on his knee with a high rise dinner on it and enough pudding to sink the Royal Yacht . . .'

Since when, I'd like to know, was it a crime *to feed* the elderly?

Joey carries on,

'Would like', he continues, as if she hadn't uttered, 'to have some help in his humble home.'

That's all. You and I would think it a simple, humane request.

'You mean as well as the entire family?' the Lady Martina raps.

She obviously doesn't know the first thing about *our* family. They think a duster is something that had a last stand at Little Big Horn.

Still Joey doesn't flicker.

'He needs,' he continues, pressing – as is said – his suit, 'he needs someone to keep it clean and tidy for him. Alas we are all weighed down with the pressures of life. The need to earn our daily loaf.'

'My tear ducts can't cope with all this emotion, Mr Boswell . . .'

Snide.

'So we thought,' still smiling and immune to her jibes, Joey continues, '. . . we, you'll understand, being . . .'

Me with cone

'The family,' Madam cuts in – as though it's a dirty word.

Yes, the family. Certainly, the family. Isn't that what your lot, MISS, the ones giving you power, keep telling us we should be concerning ourselves WITH. (I'd be no use at this. I'd never be able to control my FURY.)

But not our Joey; my Joey – the top of the hill, the pick of the bunch . . .

'Certainly. The family. We thought that we would pay half of the lady and the DHSS would pay the other half so that . . .'

'Which half do you want us to pay for, Mr Boswell?' Miss Smarty-pants cuts in. It's all right being clever when you're in work and have a retirement pension and a gold carriage clock to look forward to.

'D'you want us to pay for the half that dusts and cleans or the half that sits on its backside all day drinking coffee and putting down the neighbours?'

Well! She seems to know a lot about it, doesn't she? Is she moonlighting as a char, I wonder? Or did they teach her this interview technique at Gestapo Headquarters?

'You have read the new book of rules, haven't you, Mr Boswell?' she continues, slowly like an elocution teacher. How now brown COW . . . ?

'We don't give money away, any more,' she says. 'We lend it.'

And there's our breadwinner, unfazed throughout. A gentleman to the last. Polite, smiling and precise.

'Good,' he tells drawing himself up for the *coup de grace*, 'Then you can lend us the money to pay for half of Grandad's home help and I'll put his rent up so he can draw it from you to pay you back.'

Game, set and match.

That's our Joey.

I THANK YOU, DEAR FATHER, FOR GIVING OUR JOEY THE BRAIN OF A NOBEL PRIZEWINNER AND THE CHARM OF A DIPLOMAT. I PRAY THAT HE MAY NEVER STAND FOR PARLIAMENT BECAUSE IT WOULD BE A CRYING SHAME TO SEE SUCH A BEAUTIFUL INSTRUMENT TARNISHED. AND, DEAR FATHER, GRANT OUR JOEY A BIT OF LUCK IN HIS PRIVATE LIFE OR HIS MOTHER WILL DIE GUILTY. AMEN.

Joey Boswell's Sophisticated Cocktails

Joey has kindly contributed the following recipes. Not that we drink a lot in our house. But when we do, we do it with style.

──── A MERSEY KNEE-TREMBLER ────

(The Boswells' own Harvey Wallbanger)
(This was originally a mistake – but then all the best things in life start out as mistakes.)
Add vodka to Guinness. It gives it a kick and looks innocent.

──── A BOSWELL BLASTER ────

(This is also called a Negroni – but in Italy they don't make them as big as ours.)
A large gin, a large Campari, a large sweet Vermouth. Stir. Pour over ice and top up with soda water. Lethal.

──── A DHSS STINGER ────

A large brandy (four your nerves), mixed with an equal amount of any available liqueur (for your spirits).

──── A JOEY SURPRISE ────

(It looks like rosé, tastes like heaven and kicks like a pony.) Dry white wine, laced with vodka and campari.

──── MONGY'S REVENGE ────

(This is the one that makes safe sex really safe – it makes it impossible.)
A large measure of vodka, poured near to an open bottle of dry Martini. Topped with a twist of lemon.

Chapter Four

Joey (2): The Man behind the Mask

IF IT EVER gets to the point that my family read this book – or to be more precise, if Adrian ever reads it (which I have to admit I dread; our Adrian being what he calls 'a man of letters' might find that most of *my* letters are in the wrong place). Or if Aveline flicks through it backwards, like she does all the magazines; if Jack looks at the pictures; and Billy reads the dust jacket and then subjects it to an in-depth dinner-table review; if Grandad uses it to prop up the leg of his kitchen table (Why, I often ask myself, does that man have a kitchen? He only goes in it to pot his geraniums for the window boxes); and if Joey takes it down to the DHSS to see if he can do a deal on it with Martina. If all that happens and if on top of that a miracle occurs and Freddie even notices that I've written it, then they may all, in their different ways, protest at the fact that I am giving Joey two chapters to himself.

Well, they can all think what they like. I'm writing this and I defy anyone to fit Joey into one chapter or even an entire book. He is a very complex character.

So far, I've only attempted to show the side of him that drives a Jaguar and changes his underpants twice a day. The leather gear and the gold pen. The outward exterior; smooth, charming, bright and persuasive.

He's the only one who can tell me to shut up when Freddie's in the house and I've lost my rag again. He does it kindly and even as he's doing it, I know in my heart that he's talking sense. You could say that this entire book will be about Joey. His hand will be seen in every one of the stories; his sense; his reasoning.

But I'd be doing him less than service if I didn't try to show the other side of him. The heart of him.

How to do it, that's the problem.

Would it surprise you to know that this man – this Godfather of the Kelsall Street Mafia; this scourge of the DHSS – is a vegetarian? And that there have been two loves in his life and that both of them broke his heart?

Complex? God destroyed the mould after He made our Joey.

Joey: My favourite snap

He didn't make a big thing about becoming a vegetarian. He caused no trouble. I mean, if it had been Billy, for example, we'd have been involved in deep debate for the best part of a month and then he'd have been caught eating sausages in the back yard when he thought no one was looking. But Joey just one day stopped eating meat. He left a slice on the side of his plate and when I asked him if he was sickening for something he said yes – for man's inhumanity to the creatures of the earth. And he's never touched fish, flesh or fowl from that day to this to my certain knowledge.

Nor does he bore everybody by talking about it. He believes, I think, that we each must make up our own minds. But he'll put up a good argument if he's challenged.

He'll do it in one of two ways.

He may tell you, in frightening detail, what actually happens to the living creatures before they end up as chunks of flesh on a butcher's slab. He'll tell you how the cows are filled full of chemicals to make them bigger and chemicals to make them leaner. He'll tell you how, half an hour before they're sent to the knackers they're given a special drug to make them tender and how they're then made to remain standing while all their muscles disintegrate. He'll explain how they're then stunned and suspended upside down by a hook through the Achilles tendon and trundled towards their death.

'If you want to eat meat,' he'll tell you, 'you go ahead and eat it. But you'll excuse me if I don't want to join you.'

Joey (2)

Well, you can imagine how you want to tuck into your sirloin and three veg after a session like that, can't you?

His second ploy is just to point at our Mongy and enquire how we would like him cooked. Boiled with dumplings? Stuffed and roasted? Or minced for a shepherd's pie? Having Joey at the table can make you very uncomfortable.

All the others still eat meat, of course. But I sometimes wonder for how long, with Joey there as our conscience. He reduces Aveline to tears, Billy to argument and Adrian to flights of poetic philosophising. Only Jack, when he was at home, managed to sit through Joey's diatribes without his appetite being affected. Until, that is, the day of our Mongy's great tragedy – then he practically turned vegan as a protest against the unfairness of life. (For Mongy's great tragedy, please turn to Chapter Six.) Shifty, of course, goes on chomping away, apparently oblivious to everything that's said.

Then, of course, there's Grandad who has the appetite of a fully grown cart horse. He doesn't sit at table with us; partly because he prefers the comfort of his own home and mostly because he makes a sucking noise when he eats that would be enough to put you on a permanent diet. But a tray is taken next door to him five times a day – three main meals and two snacks. Grandad insists on everything I feed him being entirely organic and free range. Grandad remembers when there were no such things as 'free range' and 'organic'. They didn't exist because factory farming and battery houses and chemical sprays didn't exist, that's why. When Grandad was a lad, his world was all green trees, babbling brooks and little-lambs-eat-ivy. He claims he can remember a salmon swimming up the Mersey. But I can't imagine where it'd have been going; to the quiet tarns of Salford and the spawning grounds of Stockport?

Now Grandad spends most of the day reading the small print on sauce bottles. He's become something of an authority on E numbers. He would certainly vote Green, if we had a candidate. I have to get the pedigree of every egg I serve him. I have to know the entire life-story of the flour I use, from the seed to the paper bag.

SCOUSE

I have to admit that I make a very good Scouse. I got the recipe from my mother and she got it from hers. I will in time give it to Aveline – but will wait to see how her marriage develops first. Our Scouse recipe isn't the sort of thing you like giving away willy-nilly. When people ask me I simply say: Take some left over meat and make it into a stew with veg and other ingredients. When they ask what other ingredients. I look enigmatic. Lilo Lil can't make scouse. Scouse is Freddie's favourite food. You think I'm going to give that TART the secret?

—— DOMESTIC NOTE ——

It is well nigh impossible to come up with a successful vegetarian Scouse. There is no substitute for 'left-over meat' and a Scouse made with lentils is disgusting.

—— FOR MEAT-EATERS ——

Pork chops cooked in foil with mushrooms and sour cream – I add mixed herbs and a dash of mushroom relish to this and wrap each chop separately.

—— JOEY ——

Mushrooms cooked in their own juices with garlic, herbs and cream on brown rice.

—— AVELINE ——

Yoghurt or an apple or starch reduced crispbread with 0% fat cheese spread. (Or whatever other fad of the moment she is on.)

—— GRANDAD ——

Pork chop with a scrape of mustard, cooked in foil. (It's no use giving him the mushroom and cream version. He says the mushrooms are flies in the sauce and throws the whole lot in the sink.)

—— PLUS DISHES OF ——

Mashed, roast and new potatoes (you'd think they'd turn into potatoes). Carrots, two greens and a bowl of apple sauce.

—— PUDDING ——

Vanilla ice-cream, fresh raspberries (or other fruit) and brandy sauce. (Except for Aveline, who'll probably have a spoonful from each of her brothers and then go into a decline about her hips.)

A Typical Dinner Menu

Joey (2)

We don't eat goods from South Africa because of apartheid and we don't eat apples from France because we're your genuine racial chauvinists. We don't use Soy Sauce from China, because of what they've done to Tibet, and Billy read an article recently from a newspaper that was wrapping some chips about margarine being made out of axle grease, and bang went the easy-to-spread-straight-from-the-fridge facility. Which considering most of it is used on his sandwiches makes life very difficult. Personally, I think Billy's motor would benefit from a bit of axle grease, if only to get him moving. Meanwhile I wait in trepidation for the next injunction from one of them. As it is, a trip to the supermarket is like negotiating a summit conference.

Anyway, with Joey and meat it happened quietly and without any fuss. Enough, he must have thought. I won't do that any more. And that was that. Mind, he's never cooked a meal in his life. It was me that had to work out how to feed him, while continuing to accommodate the fancies and foibles of the rest of the family.

I said there's been two loves in Joey's life. There have, of course, been an alarming number of hanky-pankies. I'm glad that one can only confess to Almighty God for one's own shortcomings. If a mother was held responsible to the Heavenly Recorder for the misdeeds of her children – I'd never be off my knees and would almost certainly now be saying a Hail Mary instead of writing these words.

But there have only, so far as I know, been two real 'this is it for keeps' loves in his life. One was for Roxy Hartwell and the other was for Edgar. And before any of you rush off to tell the world that our Joey is gay, let me assure you that Edgar was an Alsatian dog.

Edgar and Joey were inseparable. That dog lived and breathed for our lad. He'd stand stock still staring at the door from the minute our Joey went out till the moment he returned. He once went away for the day to Manchester and Edgar didn't move a single paw until he returned. I had to hoover round the beast because none of us could budge him. He just stood there, head cocked, listening for Joey's footstep on the pavement outside as if all the life in him had stopped.

It was the same for Joey. Never a day went by that he didn't take him out twice, morning and evening. He had the dog sleeping in a basket at the foot of his bed, though judging by the state of his quilt it was out of the basket and onto the bed the minute the light was switched off.

And then, one day, Edgar just disappeared. Like Joey's meat eating – he just stopped; wasn't there; gone; spirited away. Joey searched every street of the area. He fly-posted the length of Liverpool; he even had a piece on Local Radio. Nothing.

It's hard to watch a grown man grieve. There was nothing we could do for him. Not that he maundered on; that's not Joey's style. I suppose you had to know him to realise that anything was up at all. But we knew.

He started going to the local dogs' home; just checking – in case in some miraculous way somebody might find Edgar and take him in. But they never did.

Joey started donating any spare cash he had to one mutt after another, giving them another day's life – but never bringing them home. It wasn't that he didn't love the dogs, of course he did, but the house was already awash with Boswells and we'd got Mongy by then. We could never fit another one in. Besides, it was Edgar he was looking for – not just any dog.

Then, a year or so back, Joey became convinced that he'd seen him again. It was as

though he was being haunted. He kept seeing this Alsatian; older now, of course, but he was convinced that it was his Edgar.

Well things came to a head on Grandad's birthday. We were all trooping into No 28 carrying the presents when Joey saw the dog again, at the end of our street . . . and he was off, like a Grand National winner.

It was his Edgar all right. He followed the dog to a house not many streets away. A nice ordinary woman let him in. He enquired after the dog and she explained that it belonged to her father. She let him look out of the back window. There was an old fella sitting in a chair, with Edgar at his feet, looking up in an adoring fashion.

It must have torn Joey apart. But he didn't let on.

Edgar

He asked the woman where her father had got the dog from; he explained that he admired the animal and was thinking of getting one himself.

She told him that she and her husband had bought it from a local pet shop. 'Not a very nice place really,' she said. The dog had been shut in a cage. 'A big animal like that in a tiny cage. It's terrible what people will do,' she said. Her father had been living in Sheffield then, and they'd taken the dog up to him – as a present, to give him some company after her mother died. Then, recently, they'd moved him in with them because he couldn't really look after himself any more. The dog had been a real nuisance since they'd arrived, always trying to get out and not settling.

'He does love him then, your father?' Joey asked her, 'He does love the dog?'

'Love him?' she'd replied. 'Look at him! That dog is all he lives for. He has all the chairs, you know. We have to make do with the floor! He's not been bothering you has he? Digging up your garden or anything?'

'No,' Joey told her. 'But I've seen him about a bit. You should keep him in more. He'll get run over.'

She promised she would. 'It's just that he hasn't settled yet,' she told Joey. 'It's all a bit strange for him. He's not used to it. But so long as he's with Dad, the dog seems to be happy. They're wonderful company – dogs,' she added, 'you should get yourself one.'

So Joey left Edgar there. He couldn't take him away from the old man and at least he knew that the dog was being looked after and was loved.

And that's all there is to tell you about Edgar – except a funny thing. He was originally going to be called Elgar – as in *Land of Hope and Glory*. But when we had his first name disc cut the man misread Joey's writing and put Edgar instead.

'Which would you rather be?' Joey asked him and his tail wagged harder for Edgar!

'All right, then – you've made your choice,' Joey said and I can see him now rubbing his hand over the dog's head and kneeling down and giving him a hug.

With Roxy Hartwell it wasn't nearly so straightforward.

In many ways it was like a hundred other stories. Boy meets girl, they fall in love, they drift apart. She gets married to someone else. The same old story. But this one could only have happened to Joey.

He told me once that all the time they were together they did nothing but row.

'What about?' I asked.

He gave me a funny sideways look that told me the answer as clear as if he'd spelt it out. The family; all of us.

The final row – when they split up is a good example.

Roxy chose to leave him at a really bad time. Mother'd just died, so Grandad was in a dreadful state. Freddie was leaving me to go to that TART, so I was in a dreadful state. And then there'd be the usual: Billy'd be doing badly at school – so he'd be upset. One of Jack's girlfriends would be playing up – so he'd be upset. Adrian'd have some nervous rash or other – so he'd be upset. And Aveline, well Aveline was trying to be a model – and that made her permanently upset.

As for Joey?

Joey would be being tugged between his loyalty to the family and his love for Roxy and longing for his own life. And, of course, we won, didn't we? The united family. Us and ours.

The bad news – taken by accident by Adrian, who was changing the film on his camera in the sitting room at the time with the door open.

But he never stopped loving Roxy Hartwell. And, in the way that fate has of turning up a real load of trouble when you least need it, she came back into his life. With one baby by the husband and another on the way, there she suddenly was, queueing at the same cash point outside the bank. Of course she loved him too. Always had. Never stopped.

I tell you, if it isn't 'hanky-panky' it's 'love' – and I'm not sure love isn't the bigger devil. You can get over 'hanky-panky', so long as you're sensible and don't contract a disease or make your partner pregnant and today we all know how to avoid that. I never thought I'd be saying this – but you can't open the paper without seeing adverts begging you to 'play safe'. It makes Grandad quite depressed. He wanted me to buy him a packet of condoms just so that he'd feel he was in the land of the living. But I have to draw the line somewhere. I don't mind getting him free range eggs but I will not encourage him to be free range himself – not at his age.

But 'love'? You can't shake love off so easily. It hangs around like a persistant cold – the kind that just when you think you're over it you start sneezing again.

For Joey, Roxy Hartwell was a permanent box of Kleenex. And, of course, she used every trick she knew to win him back. Silly lass, she couldn't see that she'd never lost him. She even went so far as to send me a note making out that Joey was the father of her child. Of course I didn't know it was from her. There was just this anonymous note thudding through our letter box along with three free soap offers and a catalogue for seeds: *Joey is the father of my child.*

Joey - the chairman of the board

It was a lovely start to the day. I showed him, of course, and he insisted that the others be told. He said he'd coped with their problems for long enough – now they could share one of his.

I had to ask him if there could be any truth in it. He looked a bit trapped and said how should he know? As though there might be a whole batch of little Joeys running about. He said he was a young man and that he'd had relationships with a few . . . The way he said 'few' wasn't very reassuring. Of course, I knew he hadn't been living the life of a monk but the vagueness of his reply shook me a bit.

But he guessed who it was from. I think in his heart he wished it was true. It wasn't, of course. It was her wish, her dream too. Funny how people go on, when they're hurting. That's what 'love' can do.

I doubt we've heard the last of Roxy even now. He can't get her out of his system. It's foolish of course, but I know it can happen. However hard we try, some of us, when we give our hearts we give them for ever. Love! Personally I'd rather have a good walk in Sefton Park.

DEAR FATHER, BLESS MY ELDEST SON, JOEY, AND KEEP HIM SAFE. LET HIM HAVE A BIT OF HANKY-PANKY FROM TIME TO TIME; AFTER ALL IF YOU CREATED THE UNIVERSE AND EVERYTHING THAT'S IN IT, YOU CREATED MEN'S URGES AS WELL – SO THEY CAN'T BE ALL SINFUL. AND, DEAR FATHER, NO ONE KNOWS BETTER THAN YOU HOW LOYAL AND LOVING HE IS TO HIS FAMILY, BUT HE NEEDS A LIFE OF HIS OWN AS WELL. LET HIM MEET SOMEBODY ELSE INSTEAD OF ROXY HARTWELL, BECAUSE THEY SEEM TO BE ALWAYS OUT OF STEP WITH EACH OTHER. FIND HIM A NICE CATHOLIC GIRL WITH A REASONABLE CHEST AND A VEGETARIAN COOKBOOK. BUT THEN, IF IT'S POSSIBLE, DON'T LET THEM MOVE TOO FAR FROM KELSALL STREET, FATHER, BECAUSE HE'S THE MAINSTAY OF MY LIFE, IS JOEY, AND THE RANGE ON THE CORDLESS 'PHONE IS LIMITED AND I DON'T MIND ADMITTING, I'D BE LOST WITHOUT HIM. AMEN.

If your nose goes red and burning, rub your ears. They say the blood rushes to your ears and leaves your nose. (This could go down as the single most useless helpful hint I've ever been given. I got it off Julie's mother, during one of her sober moments. She has a more or less permanent red nose, but that's probably because she's always too tight to find her ears.)

If a zip isn't running properly, a little soft soap or candlewax rubbed on it will have an immediate effect. (Though with my family, I've spent a lifetime searching for a way to keep the zips closed. I sometimes think the zip fastener was invented with the Boswell male in mind. At least with buttons they had to fumble a bit, which gave a woman a chance.)

To avoid soggy pastry in TARTS, sprinkle the bottom with a mixture of sugar and flour before putting in the fruit. (But of course, in our house, TARTS are banned and, besides, HER bottom is beyond redemption.)

A few drops of baby oil in the bath water stops your skin becoming dry. However, if Aveline was the last one to use the bath tie a safety belt to the door knob before getting in — she uses that much oil it's a deathtrap.

If your nylon underwear has gone grey, dye it flesh-coloured by dipping it in a strong brew of tea. Simmer, until you achieve the required colour. I read this somewhere, probably in Katie Boyle's column, but I can't say I've tried it. If ever I do, I must avoid serving the resultant tea to Grandad; he'd know at once.

To relieve a hangover, drink a lot of water before going to bed. (But this is not a good idea for the elderly. Grandad tried it and spent the night peeing out of the front bedroom window because he was too drunk to find the door and he'd drunk too much to care.)

Chapter Five

Jack

IF IT'S TRUE that absence makes the heart grow fonder then this chapter must be read bearing in mind that my second son, Jack, has been away living in America.

He's been in Los Angeles, working in a delicatessen shop owned by his cousin, Eddie, who's father, Charlie, was Grandad's brother. Eddie's not much older than Jack and very well preserved; which he would be on account of the fact that – I may as well get this over fast – Eddie, who lives in America, in Los Angeles, California, where Hollywood is, well, Eddie, well, he's gay. Not ecstatically happy, you understand, but gay. A poof. What the text books call 'a practising homosexual' (though why they have to practise, beats me. You'd think it'd be something you'd just pick up. Like playing the piano by ear). Anyway, Eddie is a pansy, as Grandad would say.

I have nothing against them. I haven't met many. I haven't had a chance to study them. In fact the only gay I've seen close to is Eddie and he seemed like everyone else, really. He's got good skin – a very good complexion, but you can't hold that against him, can you? Apart from that he just looked like one of mine.

Which is what worries me, when I think of Jack ending up going over there and living and working in close proximity with him. I know that Joey insists that you can't catch it – being gay – like an infection, but I still think you've got to be careful.

I thank God constantly that it wasn't our Adrian that went out there to work in Eddie's Deli. I mean our Adrian *is* impressionable and when he gets into one of his artistic moods he looks half-way there already; not gay exactly, but definitely cheerful. And, yes, I suppose a less likely candidate for being gay you couldn't meet than our Jack. But all the same, the customers in that delicatessen must all be of the same persuasion. They club together, don't they? They all eat their sort of food and listen to their sort of music. (I'm not sure about the food, but the music is usually Judy Garland – of whom I was once a fan. Which just goes to show how confusing life can be.) All I'm saying is, and I hope it doesn't sound prejudiced, I don't want Jack coming back with a shoulder bag and smelling of leather polish.

But to begin at the beginning with our Jack. He's the one who was born while Freddie was playing darts in Blackpool. Not that this is any explanation for his character, but at least it'll help you to place him.

School passed Jack by in a haze of rushed homework and Joey's cast-off dates. Mind, that was only when he was young and experimenting. He very soon got the hang of it in that department. His problem, always, was his soft heart. He had one girl,

Jack

Jack

Jenny Jamieson, and I swear the only reason he fell for her was that she was so plain no one else would touch her. And big? Jenny Jamieson was built like a fork lift truck. That's why I worry about him in LA. He could turn gay purely for humanitarian reasons.

His approach to his job was exactly the same. He saw himself as an antique dealer. (I'm sorry to keep harping, but a lot of them are poofs, aren't they? It's well known. 'Nice young men, in antiques.') Really he was more of a buyer and seller. His trouble was he used to buy dear and sell cheap – which can't have been how it was meant.

Jack – at home where he belongs. Taken by Adrian – you can tell he's just run back to his seat after setting the timer.

The list of his disasters would rival the Liverpool Telephone Directory. He bought a dozen radios off one shady character, and when he opened the box, there were three radios on top and a crate of apples below. We had apple crumble till it was coming out of our ears. (I even gave some to the window cleaner in lieu of a tip. He was glad of them as it happened because his wife was expecting and she had a craving for them.)

He tried to sell a bike to Father Dooley that turned out to be Father Dooley's in the first place, pinched from outside the church a fortnight before. But he's an honest boy. He would never pinch himself – and of course he didn't charge Father Dooley for returning his bike, even though he'd paid a lot for it. I suppose that might give him a few points with the Almighty, but you can never be sure.

He bought 'an old master', a picture of a nude woman that was going to make his fortune, and Julie, Billy's ex, put her fist through it. He bought a statue off a man who actually suggested an address where he could get a good price for it. Of course he could, it was one of a set of six, and the chap he'd bought it off had pinched it from there not half an hour before. There was a long line of identical statues, with a nasty little gap between number three and number five. I mean, you'd think our Jack would have thought . . . 'Funny! If this fella knows where he can get a good price for this statue – then why is he selling it to me for a song and pointing *me* in the direction of the fortune? Why isn't he going down and collecting it for himself?' But, no. Not our Jack. He's so trusting, some people feel obliged to cheat him.

That was the trouble with that line of business, of course, it attracted the less savoury elements of society. And I can't help thinking that a gay delicatessen in LA will attract the gay elements of society and, once again, our Jack has laid himself wide open to being manipulated. He's a good looking boy and he has always been very friendly.

He was the laughing one, the philosophical one. No matter what life chucked at him he'd bounce back with renewed determination. But as the years ticked by and one deal after another crumbled to dust in his hands he began to get a bit of a grudge against life. I'd always tried to teach them all that some people are born with a silver spoon in their gob and some are born with a shovel and that you have to be happy with your lot, even while you try to improve it. But Jack got the yearning to be rich – and once that gets into your bones, there's no let up. For one thing – how rich is rich? I've noticed that the very rich always think they could be richer. The very poor, on the other hand, damn well know they're poor.

Well, that's why he went to LA with gay Eddie. I expect. To make his fortune. And he has. He's really made it now, to my eternal pride. He's the first of my lot to have a high yield investment account, *in his own name.* Apparently American poofs splash their money about like they do their under-arm deodorants.

Come home, son. I wish you'd come home.

He once took our Adrian with him on a job – it was soon after Adrian was made redundant from his legitimate work and before the Muses leapt onto his shoulder and he abandoned himself to the arts. I think Jack did it out of kindness; to give his brother an occupation. Adrian did quite a few jobs with Jack, with increasingly disastrous results.

Anyway, the one I want to tell you about was to do with some hats. A collection of 1920s women's hats. An old fella was selling them – about a hundred he had. History doesn't record where he got them – but I thought the whole thing sounded highly suspect. What would a grown man be doing with a hundred women's hats? Anyway, Jack was convinced that they'd be worth a fortune and he'd already agreed a price of £15 with the old chap, so off they went to collect.

Adrian and Jack – off on another disaster.

My Jack

Arriving at the house, they were greeted by the old man's son, who, they both agreed, looked a bad lot. Well, Adrian took one look at the two boxes of hats and decided that it was daylight robbery giving the old fella only £15. That's our Adrian. We could all starve but his conscience will be unblemished. So he nagged Jack into giving a bit extra and they end up handing over £25 to the man's son. (Are you keeping track of this money transaction? We're not over yet.)

So, having paid the son, they were just setting off in the van when they saw the old man himself coming towards them down the road.

'Oh, you've come for those hats, have you?' he calls.

'S'all right, Grandad,' ever-smiling Jack responds, 'we've seen your son.'

'And there's a little surprise for you,' Adrian-the-big-hearted adds, referring to the extra tenner he forced Jack into adding to the purchase price.

'Son?' the old man said, 'I haven't got a son. I live alone,' and, as he spoke, the getaway car screeched past them and off down the road.

According to what Jack told me later, Adrian's next move went something like this:

'Oh,' cried the old man, 'he's taken me radio and 20 quid in cash . . .'

'That's all right, Grandad, we'll cover that. It's our fault – we should have known he was a burglar.'

'And me chess set and me carriage clock,' the old man wailed, warming to the subject.

'Don't worry, Grandad. You mustn't worry about a thing. We'll cover it. And, of course we won't call the police. Not if you don't want us to. Not if it upsets you . . .'

Twenty-five quid for the hats and forty quid to cover the robbery. Sixty-five quid in all, for a deal that had already been agreed at fifteen quid before they set out from the house. All Jack's money, of course. Our Adrian hadn't got two halfpennies to rub together.

That's what I mean about Jack – even his own family somehow manage to do him. Even when they don't mean to.

That's why I'm so proud of him now. God bless the poofs! They've made him a wealthy man.

Oh, that hat story didn't end there, by the way.

They went to a pub to recover, and they only went and sat down beside the robber and his mates. Or rather, Jack did. Our Adrian had decided to show his generous side and was buying Jack a drink to make up for the sixty-five quid he'd just cost him. So he's at the bar when the heavy mob tell Jack to 'move outside nice and quiet as if nothing is happening . . .'

Thank God for British Telecom, in spite of their exorbitant charges. Adrian managed to put through a call to Joey. I was in the middle of making dinner when the 'phone rang. Joey had lent his Jaguar to Billy to take Julie out – in the hope that a flash limousine might put a smile on her face. Greater love hath no man than to lend his Jaguar to a brother like Billy. But that's Joey, you see.

'It's our Adrian for you,' I tell him, passing him my cordless.

He listened for a minute, then rose, nice and calm.

'Nothing to worry about, Mam,' he said, going to the door. 'The van's broken down – Adrian and Jack want a lift home. I'm going to pick them up, OK?' and he's off out of that room, like a champagne cork.

Well, of course, he'd forgotten that he hadn't got his Jag. Rather spoilt the effect, stuttering there in Billy's VW with all the bits of string that hold it together flying behind him in the wind.

Meanwhile, I gather the heavy brigade had taken Jack to a car down a back alley and were promising to do all sorts of nasty things to him – just because he was alive and had recognised the robber.

Adrian, thinking he'd be helpful, had driven Jack's van across the alley mouth,

A Motto of Adrian's

**HE THAT GIVETH
RECEIVETH MORE.**

Jack

blocking their exit. But Adrian wasn't going to be much use if it came to a punch up, was he? I mean the power of the English language is never going to dent many heads, is it? So very wisely he just hid in the back of the van. And one of the robbers took our Jack's keys and moved it out of the way, lock, stock and Adrian covered with a dust sheet just behind the driving seat. You have to know Adrian to realise that he isn't exactly a coward. He's just artistic.

Back goes the robber to the get-away car. God knows where they were going to take our Jack – a mortuary slab, I shouldn't wonder. But, in the nick of time – like the US cavalry – in rode Joey – or rather, he fizzed and banged to a halt in Billy's car, once more blocking their exit.

Jack explained that he had a lot of brothers. But still they're not fazed. We can deal with Joey, they thought.

Jack on his own – ever hopeful

'Greetings,' he said. And he started doing a calculation:

'One radio, twenty quid. One chess set, twenty quid. One carriage clock, twenty quid. One consignment of hats, twenty-five quid. I make that eighty-five quid,' he told them. 'And let's add on another fifteen quid, inconvenience money, shall we?'

He keeps so calm, so cool, so . . . Joey.

'I think we've got a faulty brain box here, Jacko,' one of the nasties merrily quipped.

You know how at the cinema this would be the moment when our hero would whip out his marvellously concealed Colt 24 – or whatever those little shooters are called? Well, I was wrong. The English language can be powerful. It wasn't a gun our Joey produced from the inside pocket of his £250 leather jerkin, it was his cordless 'phone.

'Now let me see, what's that number again?' he asks, stabbing his finger on the 9 button three times.

And they came away with a hundred pounds – after a bit of a fight, mind. Joey told me he got his black eye fixing Jack's van. They can be very dangerous things, motors.

I thank you, dear Father, for the blessing of my son, Jack. He may not be the most diligent of church-goers, but he always speaks well of you and he tries so hard to do the right thing. Now that he's made his fortune, bring him safely home from America and, dear Father, help me to read the signs right so that if he's gay now, I can ask Father Dooley for the correct guidance. It isn't that I'd exactly mind, Father, after all, we're all your children. But for his sake, being the lad he is, wouldn't it be a bit like being our Mongy? Still as lovable as ever but every so often you can't help noticing that there's a bit missing. I think I'd rather he took up with Jenny Jamieson again than become a poof and she's bound to be free. Oh, I don't know though, imagine having her at the dinner table; I will say one thing for Eddie, he had lovely manners. If he told me once he told me a hundred times to 'have a nice day'. It became a sort of obligation, Father. I felt it was letting the side down if I didn't sparkle from morning to night. But – Jenny Jamieson! The one time she came into this house she broke the sofa. Just sat on it and snap! all four legs flew off. Well, that's no good for our Jack. He'd be better off with a nice light boyfriend than that. Oh, Father! You do move in some mysterious ways. Help me to accept whatever comes to pass. Thy will be done, Father. Amen.

Chapter Six

I HAVE DECIDED to break off from writing about the children for this brief interlude.

I want to tell you about Mongy's great tragedy. The dog hadn't been well and Joey had taken him down to the vet. It was lunchtime and I'd prepared cold ham and salad for the family and poached salmon for Mongy to cheer him up. I'd been going to do him a fillet steak but the butcher said they weren't best quality. Joey would be having cheese with his salad, I think, and maybe some rice and pineapple, dressed with walnut oil and raspberry vinegar. Because he doesn't eat meat, I like to use my imagination for him.

It was while Aveline was away, modelling, so she was spared the gory details that here follow.

We were all a bit on edge. Mongy had never been away from home before – not for any length of time. When he's courting he's in and out a lot, of course, but he never misses a meal time.

When Joey arrived back from the vet, he was without the dog. I knew at once that the news wasn't good.

'Where is he, Joey?'

'He's going to be all right . . .'

There was a lot of sighs of relief at that.

'. . . just an operation, that's all,' Joey concluded.

I felt sick.

'An operation? On Mongy?'

'What's wrong with him?' Jack asked.

'Is it serious?'

'An operation? On our Mongy?' Billy repeated. He has a habit of doing this. I think it's to give his brain a chance to catch up with reality. 'When?'

Mongy, before the great tragedy

'Tomorrow morning,' Joey replied.

'That soon?' I asked, sensing the worst.

'The vet took him in because his temperature was up – but that turned out to be nothing – anyway, while he was examining him, he found a lump . . .'

'Oh, my God – a lump,' I said, sitting down. And then I crossed myself and silently prayed. 'Is he going to die?' I asked.

Jack was getting nervous now.

'They can cope with lumps – they just turn them out – it's like shelling peas. Isn't it?' He looked at Joey, pleading with his eyes.

'Hey, come on,' Joey said, trying to calm us all. 'He's going to be all right. The lump can be removed . . . But . . .'

Now Adrian was getting into gear.

'But. I can't stand that word "But",' he wailed, wringing his hands. ' "The planet is not going to explode – BUT", "You're not going to die – BUT" . . . It means the planet isn't going to explode YET, and you're not going to die today. BUT it's going to explode tomorrow and you'll cop it then instead.'

He always uses a lot of words, does Adrian; but I did know what he meant.

'In order to do the operation successfully . . .' Joey continued.

'I'll give my blood,' I said, going to put my coat on.

'In order to succeed,' Joey pressed on, 'they'll have to castrate him.'

Funny how the bad things in life are always followed by a silence. After the bomb falls – silence. After the door slams – silence. This moment was no exception.

We all sat down again. I couldn't grasp it at first.

'You mean deprive him of his – take away his . . . ?' I fumbled for the right words.

'They can't do that, he'll look daft,' Jack protested.

'Never mind how he'll look,' Adrian was shaking now, 'what about how he feels? He's the King dog around here – he's got them all lined up. It's his right – they're taking his doghood away.'

'The thing is, it's the only way,' Joey explained. 'If Mongy is going to be free of his tumour, then he's got to part with his bits and pieces.'

'He'll get a funny bark,' I said, 'sort of soprano.'

'No, he won't,' Joey assured me. 'He won't be able to procreate, that's all. It's not the end of the world, I mean he's done it enough times to lie back and reminisce, hasn't he?'

'And anyway, it's better than being dead,' Billy added.

'I'm not so sure,' Jack said with feeling, shaking his head as he spoke.

'You're thinking like a human, Jack,' Joey told him. 'Mongy's a dog – he won't even know what's happened.'

'Won't he miss them – clanging about?'

'Look,' Joey sighed. 'If you're going to be morbid about it, it could have been incurable. I could have come home with his collar and lead, couldn't I? Let's just be thankful – OK?'

Joey was right, of course. I said grace and started serving the meal.

'We thank thee, O Lord, for the fruits of the earth, and we ask you to bring Mongy safely home to us, no matter what is missing. Amen. Some ham, Jack?'

'It's pig, isn't it? I don't see the difference between that pig and our dog.'

Mongy, after the great tragedy. (After losing his bits and pieces he's never sat upright for a snapshot again.)

'It's never stopped you before,' our Adrian told him.

'I haven't had cause to think before, have I?' Jack retorted, which wasn't strictly true.

'Animals are animals – if you eat that pig, you might as well casserole Mongy – and have Grandad's canary on toast.'

'Let's just cut out the chat and have the salad,' Joey said. It'd been a hard day for him, of course.

'I'll have your ham,' Billy said, stretching across the table to Jack's plate. 'It doesn't worry me. We have to live, don't we?'

'Isn't it funny,' Jack said, giving Billy a look, 'I wouldn't feel half so bad if someone had come home and said they were going to castrate our Billy.'

'Jack – wash your mouth out,' I told him.

'Well, he's obscene, he is. His spare parts aren't in jeopardy, are they? And look at him there, mowing his way through a cooked pig . . .'

'Leave it, Jack,' Joey cut in, 'he's just a baby lad . . .'

'A baby lad?' Now it's Adrian's turn. 'He's way ahead of the rest of us, isn't he? He spends most of his time perpetuating the human race. His spare parts will be worn out by the time he's thirty . . .'

And the usual Boswell family warfare ensued.

I was just glad that it happened when our Aveline was away, trying to be a model – though, of course, I told her about the tragedy when she telephoned.

She didn't seem too upset, but then fighting her way to the top of the modelling tree occupied all her emotional energy. She said she thought it was a routine operation. Well, so it was, I suppose. But Mongy was very well endowed. It can't have been easy for him. I mean, if you suddenly take a cup off a full tray – well, it sort of tips up, doesn't it?

WE THANK THEE, DEAR FATHER, FOR ALL THE LITTLE CREATURES AND THE WILD ANIMALS AND MOST PARTICU-LARLY FOR MONGY. I HOPE HE DOESN'T MISS HIS BITS AND PIECES AND THAT, WHEN HE IS EVENTUALLY CALLED TO THE GREAT KENNEL IN THE SKY, HE HAS THEM REINSTATED. AMEN.

Chapter Seven

Adrian

THE FIRST THING you should know about Adrian is that he isn't Adrian at all; he's Jimmy. James was the name he was given in the sight of God and Jimmy he was called by all the family until he got it into his head that it didn't 'go with his image and would we please call him Adrian from now on'.

Maybe it's difficult – being in the middle. With two older brothers and a younger sister and brother he's bound to feel something of a misfit and an in-between. For this reason maybe, Adrian – because we all do as we're told and call him that, except when we forget or are annoyed with him – has always been both a trier and a worrier. He's the only one of them that actually worked at schoolwork at school. Joey breezed through on charm and an agile mind. Jack slogged away and got his girlfriends to do his homework. (Which is a clear explanation of why he consistently got low grades; Jack wasn't inclined to pick his female company for their intellectual abilities. Like his father before him he has always been sadly inclined to the grotesque sweater line.) Aveline never thought it necessary to dazzle with the mind when she could do so with her looks and from an early age she relied on her body to do the talking. And Billy – well, all I can say about Billy and school is that they were not compatible. But I will eventually come to Billy and try to explain the almost unexplainable, so for the moment let me simply say that he suffered more at school, for less results, than seems humanly possible.

But Adrian got stuck in there and in no time he was sitting his A Levels and passing – though what use A Levels in English literature, History, Art and Botany was going to be to a young man setting off on life's long voyage through urban Liverpool in the '80s was and remains a mystery to me.

However Adrian is 'A for Application'. He went out there and got himself a job. I remember his coming back all flushed with success and announcing to a stunned family gathered round the table as usual (our family only ever seem to meet with their noses in the trough), that he was going into 'Real Estate'.

There was a lot of debate about whether Unreal Estate wouldn't have been more profitable – but, of course, we were all proud of him. Not that he seemed to earn much from Real Estate. His first month's wages went on buying a leather briefcase which I think he must have had grafted to his right hand, because you never saw him without it from that day on. Oddly enough, the day he got that briefcase was the day he stopped carrying what was left of his comfort blanket like a sodden little ball in his pocket. And he got in a terrible state about that. He couldn't find it and he'd wanted to put it in the briefcase. I told him it was a shame to spoil the leather interior trim with a mangled little ball that had been sucked and chewed since he was a baby; but apparently I didn't understand its 'true significance' nor did I appreciate its 'symbolic stature'. We searched high and low for it but to no avail. Adrian kept yelling that his 'peace of mind was hanging by a thread' but then he's always got something or other hanging by a thread, be it his sanity or his masculinity or even his life, so we didn't get too alarmed. We never did find that comfort blanket but I did catch a contented look on Mongy's face and that dog will eat anything he finds lying on the floor. That's why I never have people camping out on the sitting room carpet, he'd have them for breakfast.

After the initial purchase of the briefcase the most he managed to put in the family pot was the odd pound coin; apparently, working in Real Estate you have a lot of outlay, mainly on things to put in your briefcase I think.

Eventually the bottom fell out of Real Estate, or something like that, and our Adrian was made redundant. He was devastated, of course. But then everything devastates Adrian and it's best not to get caught up in his emotional vortex (his words to describe what used to be known as a paddy).

We told him that now he was a real part of the family business and that being in Real Estate had been stifling his natural talents. He seemed to accept this without a murmur though at that time none of us had really defined what his natural talents were and I was only saying it to encourage him (funny how, later, I was to be proved right). Joey took him down to the DHSS to introduce him to Martina – our personal counter clerk – and to sign on.

Our Adrian trying to charm Martina at the DHSS – recorded for posterity by Joey, with a camera hidden in his leather jacket.

Adrian – before he went too artistic

58

Adrian

Martina, apparently, was less than thrilled to discover another Boswell hammering at her gates. I've only met her once and I didn't take to her. She has the attitude of Marie-Antoinette about her, as though she's thinking all the time 'let them eat cake'. She'd be advised to remember what happened to Marie-Antoinette. The chop is waiting round the corner for the most unlikely people. This may sound ungracious of me but, as I stated earlier, this woman – this public servant, this DHSS employee put there by us, the public, to serve us and do our bidding (well, how else can you define a civil servant?) – had the lack of finesse to fall for Shifty Boswell (of whom you will no doubt hear later, unless I can avoid the subject), and as such I cannot treat her to too much credibility.

I exempt Celia Higgins, my friend and neighbour, from this judgement. She also fell for Shifty, but she's a woman of the world and probably knew what she was doing and what she hoped to get out of it. Also, of course, all women were born fools where men are concerned, and I include myself in that category. There's always some top heavy tart waiting to take your man when you're least expecting it.

At least Martina has had the sense to have a special filing cabinet, marked 'BOS-WELL', installed in her office in which to keep our personal dossiers, which shows not only the kind of impression we've made on her but also what can be achieved if you really put your heart and soul into a job, like Joey has done with the Department of Health and Social Security over the years. He has quite simply become a virtuoso of the sub-clauses and a master of the printed form. Before him a minion like Martina can only cringe and surrender. The fact that he doesn't always score is due entirely to red tape and not to any proficiency on her part – mind, I am Joey's mother and I may therefore be showing some bias in this matter.

Our Adrian didn't take at all easily to Unemployment. Some do, some don't. None of us want it, of course. But the last thing you can do is mope about, getting depressed. You have to go out there and beat them at their own game.

As mentioned previously, Jack took him on a few jobs, but it wasn't a happy arrangement. I think the trouble was that Adrian brought his Real Estate mentality to bear in an area where, perhaps, natural low cunning was what was called for. But then, to be reasonable, I think the same low cunning is required in Real Estate as well – which could explain why Adrian got the pot handshake. Pot indeed. You *hear* of people being made redundant, getting golden ones and walking away with fortunes but I've never met anyone who actually has. But then I've never met anyone who's won one of those competitions you get on the sides of packets. 'Name three vegetables beginning with the letter C; and state in not more than ten of your own words why Doggy-Bix is your favourite pet food and win the holiday of a lifetime for two at the fabulous Caesar's Palace in Las Vegas . . .' Have you ever met anyone who's been for a fabulous holiday to Las Vegas, free? Or flown Concorde? Or even won the jackpot at Bingo? Because I haven't.

What Adrian requires, I realise now, is a framework. That's why he was good at school. He had somewhere to go in the morning. That's why he fitted into Real Estate. He's no good at hanging around waiting to see what'll turn up. He has to have an image to relate to, a place to report to, a persona to live up to; schoolboy, Real Estate agent, poet, artist, great lover.

So, very soon, without the office to go to each morning, he began to see the gaps in

Mrs Boswell's Slice of Bread

his life – and, God help us, he began to fill them.

The biggest gap – like a black hole, really – was 'Love'. Not for our Adrian something common like 'hanky-panky'. He had to have 'Love'. And, poor lad, he had to go and meet, and hope to find it with, a rampant carnivore by the name of Carmen. Carmen! I ask you. She was one of those who'd had nothing but salads all her life and was on the look out for a hot dinner – and she chose our Adrian?

It was all passion and heavy breathing with those two from the first day. We know because she phoned him up once, when we were in the middle of supper and there he was all pale and quaking, promising to wear his brown cords again. Brown cords? What did she think he was? Lady Chatterley's Lover?

Oh, our Adrian! It's hard to stand by and watch your own flesh and blood being eaten alive. Needless to say it got our Jack very worked up – because she sounded just the sort of girl he'd been searching for. And even our Joey betrayed a gleam in the eye that wasn't exactly fraternal.

Carmen, a TART-in-the-making, is the blonde in the middle. Billy's Julie doesn't look too happy – but then she never does.

Adrian

A lot of what took place between Adrian and Carmen should have been no more than mere speculation to us all, but of course Adrian always came home with either his virginity or his virility hanging by a thread and we'd be subjected to the lurid details over our chicken chasseur. I could draw a map of the bushes they tried 'hanky-panky' behind, not to mention the beauty spots of England that they climbed, crossed or burrowed beneath in their desperate desire to fulfil their carnal passion. If they'd managed it once then I expect they'd have erected a monument to commemorate the event. But there are no monuments – they talked about it so much that I doubt there was ever enough passion left to erect anything of much significance.

I knew things were getting to a drastic state when he brought home a book from the library entitled *How To Gain Confidence*.

Our Jack came to the rescue and tried to advise him, but being Jack he didn't use kid gloves. He just leapt in and told him straight that he didn't need a book:

'Sex', he explained, 'is nature's trick, Adrian. It's just bodies – it's fun. It's getting it right and getting it wrong and laughing all the way.'

Funny how assured you can be when it isn't your problem. I've seen our Jack knotted up with nerves over a woman many times.

'I'd like to talk about love rather than sex, if you don't mind,' Adrian told him, masking his embarrassment behind a snooty look.

'Ah, yeah, "love",' Jack agreed, looking haunted. 'Well, that's different. That's more to do with brain damage, terminal lunacy and a lot of sobbing.'

'Well, your experiences have obviously been more ecstatic than mine,' Adrian countered, 'and anyway, I can't understand why you're so cynical about everything. I mean, look at last year, all your conquests.'

'It was a good year, last year.'

(Jack has never been a slave to modesty.)

'Elaine Shardley, Jean Connaught, Lizzie Haycroft . . .'

It was true, he did have a string of females after him.

'And Brenda Makin, don't forget Brenda Makin . . .'

'Well, there you are!' Adrian cries, making a broad gesture with his arms – maybe next time round he should try being an actor. He's definitely got the dramatic streak. 'You must've been getting something right. Unlike me.'

So – Jack deduces that his brother must be frightened of women and decides to set him right. The things you hear when you're stuffing a cabbage. But:

'No,' Adrian protests. 'Women are wonderful . . .'

Actually, Adrian, should you ever ask me – your Mother – I can name one or two who are distinctly NOT wonderful. However:

'No,' he continues, 'it's Carmen I'm frightened of.'

'A bit of a goer, isn't she?' Jack is nodding now, very man of the world. 'Jean Connaught was like that. I used to plan quiet evenings sitting in the back of the van with a bottle of Blue Nun and a box of Milk Tray but she had my shirt undone before I could get the top off the bottle.'

'That's it! That's just how it is!' Adrian exclaims, overcome with masculine buddiness. 'Oh God, that's just how it is. All physical.'

'I've been there. I've been there,' Jack nods wisely in agreement.

'I don't get a chance to talk,' Adrian is now sobbing with frustrated bonhomie, 'to think, to plan. Two minutes after we meet, she's checking my erogenous zones.'

'They have a knack, don't they?'

'That's it, that's it. They have a knack!'

It's as exciting as Stanley discovering Livingstone in the middle of the jungle. They're hugging each other now mentally as they share the pain of being lusted after.

'Then it's the kiss and the whisper, then it's the eyelashes. Oh, God, the eyelashes. Then it's the little wiggle . . .'

'It's good news, the little wiggle,' Jack yells. 'When the little wiggle comes – you're nearly there.'

'And the next thing you know . . .'

'You're banging away like a couple of road drills, I know. I've been there. Great, isn't it?'

No, Jack – you just blew it. Can't you see? That's how it may be for you – but it's just how it isn't for our Adrian. When he gets to that point, he wants to 'think', to 'talk', to compare what's happening to him to what happens in Shakespeare's sonnets, and little bells ringing and buttercups after rain. In other words – he's dead scared.

Nor is he going to be helped by Billy telling him that sex is like eating jelly babies – and I'm glad he stopped him from explaining precisely what he meant, because I don't think I'd have liked it nor would I have wanted to impart the information here.

Not that I'm blaming Carmen really. She did try, so far as I can gather, to build his confidence. She told him he was a tiger and that he set her world on fire and all the other things people whisper while they're trying to unfasten buttons. It's just that he knew that there had to be more to it than he was actually achieving. That's the wonderful thing about nature. We get up in arms about sex education – but there's a little voice in the head that tells you if you've passed. You don't need your A Levels for that.

What Adrian found hard was – being a man. Just that. He found it very hard – being a man. But as Joey pointed out to him he was too much of a perfectionist.

'We all have to learn – about everything,' he told him. 'Leonardo da Vinci drew arms and legs before he painted the Mona Lisa.'

I rather think that was intended to make Adrian feel secure and confident – like being back at school doing biology. And I can see that his attitude had a hint of the classroom about it. A sort of analytical approach to 'hanky-panky'; like:

'When you're a boy you worry about when you're going to do it. When you're a man you worry about how you're going to do it. And when you've done it you worry about how everybody else does it.'

Well, of course he finally managed it – much to the relief of us all. And when he'd done it he followed some advice from Joey and he walked away. He just upped and left her. She must have thought: At last! Eureka! We've done it! He managed it! He was a tiger! The earth moved! And Adrian just snapped his fingers at her, pulled up his trousers, walked away and before she had time to button her blouse, he was off on his bike without *once* looking back. I had to admire that . . .

Though, of course, Father, I don't really approve of all this 'hanky-panky', but what am I to do? Boys have to get it out of their systems. I just wish you'd devised some less untidy method of doing it and I also wish you'd created a breed of females who didn't complicate it even further with their constant demands for earth moving and soul shattering. It's quite enough to be forever crawling in and out of your clothes without

Adrian, the poet. Broken, but please Father, not bent.

having to be subjected to psychiatric analysis as well.

But did I not say early in this chapter that our Adrian is A for Application? He didn't let the grass grow under his feet for long.

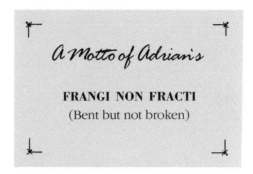

A Motto of Adrian's

FRANGI NON FRACTI
(Bent but not broken)

Dear Father, I don't like the use of that word 'bent'. Does a mother ever stop worrying, Father? Is there ever an end to it?

Having conquered the art of consummated seduction, our Adrian passed on to higher things. He decided to apply himself to more cerebral pursuits than mere bonking. He started writing poetry instead.

I know, I know. I can hear the groan from Land's End to John O'Groats. Poetry?

But this is Adrian I'm talking about – four A Levels and a bookcase of his own. I daresay a lot of young people write poetry. But not all of them get it published, do they? Adrian did. We've each got a copy. It was an anthology of Northern writers:

PARTING

by

Adrian Boswell

I do miss you

This feeling of one

Not that love was spoken

But it was done

The silent moving

Of me and you

Silken sheets and perfumed oil

I miss that too

Selected Poems from the North, page 27. Poems by Adrian Boswell. 'My Granny's Bucket', 'Go Now', 'Arthritic City'; I don't know where he gets the words. Even one about our Mongy – 'Dog'. Then there was 'Parting':

I don't know where he gets the ideas from either. Silken sheets? The only time he was ever indoors with Carmen was in Grandad's front room – and there are no silken sheets there; nor was there any 'hanky-panky', not with Grandad coming in every three minutes to water his aspidistra.

I suppose it's creative inspiration. Like living with John Keats or Alfred, Lord Tennyson. I don't suppose Keats ever heard a nightingale, not stuck in London; and if Alfred, Lord Tennyson really heard the 'horns of Elfland faintly blowing' he'd have ended up working in a delicatessen in Los Angeles! Have a nice day indeed.

It's odd when one of your own flesh and blood suddenly comes out with something like poetry and gets it printed and becomes a celebrity. In a way I felt I'd lost him. Up until then I thought I'd had a pretty good idea what went on inside his head; I thought I understood him; I thought I knew his cravings and that we shared more or less the same ideas. But 'silken sheets' and 'My Granny's Bucket' might just as well have come from Outer Mongolia as Kelsall Street – it was suddenly all foreign. I was proud of him – my son, the poet – but I knew I'd never quite understand him again. And, what was worse, of course, I never had. Because that poetry was always lurking in there, waiting to jump out onto the printed page.

Mind, Adrian's been an encouragement, even an inspiration to me. If it hadn't been for him, I doubt I'd now be sitting here at the kitchen table with my user-friendly word processor, when there's a whole stack of washing waiting to be tumble dried.

He was that chuffed when he got the copies of his poetry book from the publisher. We each got a copy and a present. He gave me a little gold cross that I've worn ever since. There was a medallion for Mongy with writing on it: 'If you love something, let it go free. If it comes back it's yours. If it doesn't, it never was.' It was a lovely sentiment, but we kept his usual disc on his collar as well; just our 'phone number and the name 'Mongy' seemed more useful if he went missing. That's one of the problems about poetry and the poetic mind – it's not always very practical. He gave Billy a nine carat gold watch. It wasn't an entire success. Billy turned into the speaking clock and kept us informed about every passing second. Jack of course was in America, but I know Adrian sent him a copy, because he sent a postcard of The Golden Gate with the cryptic message: 'Great, our kid. Sock it to 'em.' Aveline got a pair of earrings she'd admired in a shop window and Joey got an antique pair of lorgnettes. A strange choice, I have to admit. I can't see our Joey down the DHSS flashing out his lorgnettes and giving Martina a withering look – like the Scarlet Pimpernel. But there, that's Adrian's artistic temperament again, I suppose.

And now he's taken up painting, as well. He says he's 'a true Renaissance Man'. He did our Grandad a lovely Green picture for his birthday. With trees in it – at a distance. You need binoculars to see them, but they are there. He sees himself as Leonardo da Vinci one day and William Shakespeare the next.

But he still can't get it right on the home front. A young fan seduced him only recently. Nice looking girl, apparently; she'd read his poems and thought he sounded fantastic. She wrote him a fan letter, suggesting they should meet.

Adrian – giving the thumbs up to this book.

Adrian

Dear Adrian Boswell,
I am an art student. The other day a friend of mine gave me a copy of a book of poems in which I found your work. I am writing to say how I appreciate the poems, and how I identify with them. Is it possible for us to meet? I will be outside the Everyman Cafe on Wednesday at 12.30. If you can't make it, I'll understand.

Love Ellie

Can't make it? Try and stop him!

He couldn't wait! Hot shower, body splash, a ton of talc, after shave on his arm pits and a song in his heart. The works. He was breathing so fast with excitement, I was afraid he was hyperventilating and told him to stick his head in a brown paper bag.

But no:

'I had six months with Carmen – the school of life. I'm ready for anything. I know now. I know about women. They like passion. Well it's common logic really, isn't it? I mean if God wants the universe to continue . . . Well, I mean it's no good putting a train on the track without an engine in it, is it?'

My Jimmy, in the old days, when we were full of hope and Mongy was still complete.

Oh, Adrian, love. How did you end up so artistic and so . . . hopeless? I mean – what went wrong, Adrian? How did it come about that you had to creep home down our street wearing nothing but a bin liner after one meeting with a female fan? How? You should never leave your clothes unattended when you're in the company of strangers.

DEAR FATHER, BLESS AND KEEP MY SON, ADRIAN – WHO YOU KNEW FORMERLY AS JIMMY. HELP ME, FATHER, NOT TO FEEL THAT I'VE UTTERLY FAILED HIM. GRANT HIM THE POWER TO BE A CREATIVE ARTIST WITHOUT HAVING TO GO RIGHT ROUND THE BEND. AND, DEAR FATHER, IF IN YOUR WISDOM YOU COULD FIND A WAY TO GET HIM WITH A SUITABLE GIRL IT WOULD BE A GOD SEND. (LITERALLY.) I KNOW I SHOULDN'T ASK YOU TO INTERCEDE FOR REASONS OF 'HANKY-PANKY', FATHER, BUT THINK OF IT THIS WAY. IF OUR ADRIAN COULD ONLY GET TOGETHER WITH A NICE, QUIET RESPECTABLE CATHOLIC GIRL WHO LIKES A GOOD READ AND THE ODD EVENING OUT AT A SUB-TITLED FILM, IT MIGHT SAVE HIM FROM BECOMING A POOF OR, WORSE, AN ACTOR. I MEAN, HE'S BEEN A POET, HE'S BEEN A PAINTER. I KNOW THE SIGNS, FATHER. HE EVEN DABBLED WITH BEING A MALE MODEL ONCE – WELL, YOU MUST REMEMBER, AFTER ALL, YOU CREATED HIM. BUT I CAN'T FACE HIM LEARNING LINES IN OUR SITTING ROOM AND WEARING MAKE UP AND STARING AT HIMSELF IN THE MIRROR ALL THE TIME. BESIDES, THERE'S SCARCELY ENOUGH ROOM IN OUR BATHROOM AS IT IS, WITHOUT HIM CLUTTERING IT UP WITH HIS GREASEPAINT AND HIS WIGS. IF IT ISN'T TOO MUCH TO ASK, FATHER, PLEASE, HEAR MY PRAYERS. MAKE ADRIAN NORMAL. AMEN.

Aveline was very touched by this poem, of course. But Adrian read it to her as she was getting into her frock on the morning of her wedding, which made her seem a bit unappreciative. We could none of us really concentrate on it. I suppose that's what it must be like for royalty when the Poet Laureate pops round to spout an ode – just when they're in the middle of delivering the heir to the throne or opening their pressies on a birthday. They also must feel like saying: 'Very nice, thank you. But not just at present, love.' There was actually more of this poem – but we just hadn't got time to hear it, and he threw it away in a fit of poetic temperament.

This poem was, I should think, inspired by his experiences with Carmen. He was always either loving or hating her.

FOR MY SISTER ON HER WEDDING DAY

Remember the fragile days
When you and I played
And nothing beset our minds
Except chasing butterflies
And so with life's hallmarks on your brow
It comes to now
Your wedding day.

IF YOU WERE DEAD

If you were dead I'd long to see you
I'd wander through yesterday's places aching
I would carry your face in my eye
And see nothing else
And all of me would be breaking
If you were dead there would be a death in me
I would keep your touch in my mind
Endlessly
But you're alive and I hate you.

MY GRANNY'S BUCKET

In the cobbled streets
Where the sun played
And insects hung
Like little bits of silk
Above the marigolds
I heard the sound of my Granny's bucket
As she scrubbed the step
And made it white with stone

Soft stirrings
Beneath stones
Amongst ivy
In the wash-house
Things that fluttered
And crawled
Unmolested – in the cobbled yard
To the sound of Granny's bucket.

MAGDELANA

Sweet Latin maid with darkest eye
and jet braid.
Bring your bell-like voice to my ear.
My soul is smiling now that you're here.

I had to include this poem from his published works – because it makes me cry. I'm not sure that mother actually used a bucket much, but I expect that's what's called 'poetic licence'. Fancy him seeing our backyard and our wash-house as places to write about. Sometimes now, when I catch him watching me – say when I'm drying Freddie's socks in the oven – it makes me shudder to think what one day he'll say about me in blank verse.

Apparently this brief little ditty was composed while he was getting ready to go out with the chambermaid at the Hotel Flaminio, in Rome. Being Adrian nothing happened with the chambermaid – which I think is reflected in the poem. Poor Adrian. I sometimes think he'll go to his grave with a 'smiling soul' and unfulfilled urges.

Chapter Eight

Aveline

I HAD A dream once. Well, I've had lots of dreams, but this one was so vivid that I've never forgotten it. It was the sort that, when I woke up, I thought for a minute it must be true. But it wasn't, needless to say. If it had been I'd have been a happy woman, instead of which the cold light of dawn reminded me that I was the usual worried one.

A lot of my worries have been on account of my only daughter, Aveline, and many of the dreams, including the one I am about to relate, have been to do with her as well.

I suppose it's natural that a mother should feel a closeness with a daughter and look to see in her her own departed youth. I must admit that when I look at Aveline I wish I was young again – if only because she might be a bit more inclined to listen to me. I might have been able to prevent her making some of the mistakes that she has. But then, would I have listened? When I was her age, I was already firmly pinned in that famous wrestler's grip called 'holy wedlock' with Freddie Boswell – three penalties and a warning and flat on my back on the mat – so I doubt I can claim to have made a better job of youth than she has.

But a mother can dream; and I had such high hopes for our Aveline. The particular vision I want to tell you about went something like this:

It's a Sunday morning and the butler has brought up the papers with my breakfast tray and as I idly flick through the pages of the supplements I come across this article. There's a luscious big colour photograph of our Aveline, looking stunning, lying back in a tub full of suds, in our bathroom. So I settle my head back against the pillows, sip my coffee, and read the following:

ROOM OF MY OWN – AVELINE BOSWELL

My favourite room is the bathroom at my mam's house, No 30 Kelsall Street, where I live with my brothers and sometimes my Dad if he's at home. Here I spend many long hours making myself look fabulous before going out to face the harsh world of the photographer's studio or the catwalk. It might be the front cover of Vogue *one day or a promo to the Emmanuels another. Maybe Yves has given me a bell and asked me to*

ROOM OF MY OWN
AVELINE BOSWELL

My favourite room is the bathroom at my mam's house, No 30 Kelsall Street, where I live with my brothers and sometimes my Dad if he's at home. Here I spend many long hours making myself look fabulous before going out to face the harsh world of the photographer's studio or the catwalk. It might be the front cover of *Vogue* one day or promo to the Emmanuels anoth⌐ Maybe Yves has given me a bell asked me to nip over to Paris – m ond home – to help him get his Collection off the ground⌐ Aveline Boswell wears tod⌐ couture by Friday and rea⌐ street via pirated design⌐ ing Monday fortnigh⌐ my life as glamour But it isn't like ⌐ being a top mo⌐ gorgeous ever⌐ it's here, in⌐ relax an⌐ belie⌐ the⌐

nip over to Paris – my second home – to help him get his Spring Collection off the ground. What Aveline Boswell wears today is haute couture by Friday and reaches the high street via pirated designs by the following Monday fortnight. People think of my life as glamour, glamour, glamour. But it isn't like that. It's really tough being a top model and having to look gorgeous every minute of the day and it's here, in our bathroom, that I like to relax and take time to meditate. I really believe in all that. It does wonders for the ageing process; and even I have to keep a sharp look out for all those little wrinkles that come and wander over your face, making it look like an Ordnance Survey map. So it's into the bathroom and down to the hard work of keeping fabulous. I like to get it all steamy and heavy with the smell of the perfume of my choice: Elizabeth Taylor's 'Poison' is the one I am using at the moment. After a good soak in Ginseng bath lotion, I use a body scrub, a body rinse, a body re-vitaliser and a nice splash of body oil . . .

So much for dreams – they take the truth and tart it up a bit. Aveline could have made the front cover of *Vogue* if only she'd stuck to her dreams. Instead she's in a cold Protestant vicarage, married to Oswald. What price now all that scouring and rubbing and slapping and dusting?

Aveline – with her body saying Hello

Our Jack once made the observation that the average body grows a new skin every seven days, but that his sister has to get hers every half-hour. And it's true. She's scrubbed and loofahed and rubbed at herself that hard that I used to think one day she'd disappear. She'd quite simply have erased herself. There'd be nothing left except a moist footprint on the lino to show where she once had stood.

When Aveline lived at home, you'd have been excused for thinking that she had two rooms of this house entirely to herself. She had her bedroom of course. She was the only one of the children to have a room of her own. But then, I thank God, she was my only daughter. I don't think my nerves would have stretched to a second one. And you'd have been forgiven for thinking that she also had the bathroom to herself. She seemed to spend more time in there than anywhere else. The only chance I had to get a bath was in the middle of the night, when the others were sleeping off the rigours of the day. In the morning, there was a permanent queue outside the door. It was some-how never questioned that Aveline, being a model, had a priority claim. Then Joey took second call, because he also has to look gorgeous for his work. (You can't charm the birds off the trees looking like a tailor's dummy can you? Joey's sort of style takes time and effort as well.) Next would come Adrian, who just goes in for a straight rub round and a splash of after shave (unless he's trying for a new conquest, in which case he takes an afternoon booking and comes out looking bloated from the hot water; which probably saps his strength, come to think of it); next in line would be Jack, who only really believed in washing the bits that showed; and finally there's Billy, who seems to think that looking round the door at the basin is all that's required and that in some mysterious way actually walking into the bathroom, turning round, and walk-ing straight out again is equal to the most expensive category of car wash.

Actually, to be fair, Billy sometimes claimed that he got a shower over at Julie's house. But I'm not at all sure that that was for reasons of cleanliness. There was always a smirk on his face when he mentioned it which belonged more to the adverts for Badedas than Lifebuoy Soap.

On the mornings that Aveline stripped her legs, our entire work force was likely to be late for appointments; and 'a mud pack and facial' evening could seriously jeopardise the drainage system of the entire neighbourhood – more oil and silt goes down the plug hole then than would pollute Morecambe Bay.

But then, God made her beautiful and he gave her five adoring males (four broth-ers and a father) to constantly remind her of the fact. Six, if you count Grandad – but he claims that all the scent she sprays on herself gives him asthma and, besides, he's not given to paying compliments. He says at his age any undue show of emotion is bad for his biorhythms.

It seemed pre-ordained that Aveline should work with her body; like carpenters work with their hands and accountants with their pocket calculators. If you grow up looking like Aveline, you're not going to become an atomic scientist, are you? You're going to be something up front: a receptionist or on the checkout at Tescos – some-thing where your looks speak for you. Aveline's looks say: 'Hello, I spent seven hours in the bathroom this morning specially so that I could sit in this bikini, smiling warmly while selling this brand new Porsche, in the middle of this freezing cold trade hall.'

It's the fact that her body says 'Hello' so cheerfully and so often that has given me so many sleepless nights. I'm either awake worrying about her or asleep dreaming about her.

Aveline

'You don't have to be so friendly with your body, Aveline,' I used to tell her. I'd see her strutting down the street in her high heels with her skirt up round her midriff and her knickers flashing. 'It isn't decent,' I'd tell her.

'Oh, Mam!' she'd laugh. 'It's the fashion, isn't it?'

Since when has fashion been allowed to be the cause of cardiac arrest in elderly men and incitement to rape in the younger members of that sex?

I never once saw her walking away from me without I had to cross myself and whisper a prayer of protection to St Christopher.

Aveline – with a prayer of protection from me

That's why I bought her a whistle and insisted on her wearing it on a chain round her neck whenever she went out of the house. It's not just that the streets are dangerous nowadays; she didn't realise the impression she was making.

Of course in one way we were lucky. Most of the men she worked with were the type that bottle their own jam – but she still had to get to the studio to start working with them, didn't she? There are a lot of funny people out there just waiting for an innocent girl in Dayglo tights and Lurex hot pants.

She was once mugged, actually, practically outside this door. Fella only took her handbag – but it could have been her virginity as well. Then where would we have been? From then on I tried to make her carry the cordless 'phone in her shoulder bag and take Mongy on the lead. One whiff of trouble and she was to set Mongy on the brute, blow her whistle, and then dial 999 double-quick. But she didn't like the arrangement. She said Mongy wasn't a designer dog.

'Designer dog? You've been mugged, Aveline. Mugged!'

'Oh Mam,' she protested, 'he only took my handbag. He got away with nothing but my eye liner and some glitter dust, a spare pair of tights, a jar of Evening Primrose, some false finger nails, eye lashes and a hair piece. A packet of cotton buds, some of the Queen Mother's eye drops to make me eyes sparkle, a safety pin and a tube of those little mints with the hole on account of me diet. It's all replaceable – and we'll get it off the insurance, Joey'll see to that.'

She's very thorough, is Aveline, when it comes to the tools of her trade.

But there are other ways a girl like her can be taken advantage of – and one of the most dangerous is professionally. That's her Achilles heel, that's where she was most vulnerable. She wanted so much to succeed at her chosen vocation, I used to dread passing the newsagents for fear of seeing her revealing her all from the lurid cover of some chest magazine. I used to skip page three in the Littlewoods catalogue, I was so worried. I mean, I know she's a good, sensible girl – but the desire to make it to the big time can corrupt the strongest character. We must never forget that Marilyn Monroe went nude on that calendar before she was an international movie star and that Samantha Fox has become a household name with nothing more to offer than a grotesque bosom and no shame. How could I hope that Aveline wouldn't succumb?

Joey once challenged her on this point.

'My body's in no danger,' she told him. 'I mean the family will see to that, won't they? Apart from having to wear a whistle round my neck – if I'm two minutes late coming home, you all leap into your cars. I could have been engaged to Gavin Hughes now if you hadn't all frightened him to death, jumping out at us every time we were alone together.'

Gavin Hughes? He was no good to her. And Joey told her so. All Gavin Hughes did was go round cutting people's hedges.

'He had no ambition, Princess. He declared everything!'

'He had his own hedge cutters.'

Oh, Aveline – is that all you hoped for out of life? A boy with his own hedge cutters?

'You know, Princess,' Joey told her, 'you don't have to do any job, not if you don't want to. We've got everything in our house – nobody goes short – we're family.'

But she was sick of that word 'family'. She wanted to get her own things.

'I want Janet Reger underwear, a Gucci bag, a Cartier watch. I want to walk in the wind with all me Harrods labels showing.'

And what about her pride?

'Where does pride get you?' she asked. 'Me Grandad's pride landed him in a wicker chair outside the same house he was born in. And me Mam's reward for a lifetime of pride is to end her days having a heavy relationship with a microwave.'

Huh! I haven't ended my days yet, if you must know, Princess. And there are things that I've done about which you know nothing at all. The young? They make you want to spit sometimes, forgive me Father – but, really!

Yet, of course, what she said was right. Our Aveline's body was more heavily guarded than the crown jewels. For a fella to get to see so much as her elbow was like forcing his way into Fort Knox. The boys were always there, watching and waiting; and of course, they'd been so successful with their own conquests over the years – with the exception of Adrian – that they knew all the tricks.

Aveline brings Oswald home – note the damp, Proddy smile.

One time, a nasty little individual called Monsieur André thought he'd do a few tasteful pictures of her in the altogether reclining on a couch with draped silk everywhere. Some hope! He found himself faced by the entire Brotherhood; Joey, Jack, Adrian and Billy. They stripped him of every stitch he was wearing and took a few art pictures of their own:

Mrs Boswell's Slice of Bread

'Wet your lips, André. Chin up – down a little. Sexy smile. Look at the lens, there's a good boy. Arms out – oh, yes. Very nice – pretend you're running through a field of corn. Wonderful. Fantastic, André. Oh, you look beautiful when you're angry . . .'

But there were other times, weren't there, Princess? Don't you tell me there weren't. You may have thought that your big brother, Joey, bought out every copy of that magazine from our newsagents – but he didn't check the dentist's waiting room, did he? And I dread to think how many people saw it in there. Such a sweet, innocent smile on

How it was.

How it could have been.

your face, Aveline – and your chest hanging out beneath it, shining in the light like a baby's bottom. I don't blame you, I know the temptation. Your mind said 'No'; your bosom said 'Why not?' and your ambition said 'OK, so long as Mam never finds out.' Well, I didn't let on that I had. Why put the cover on the cage when the canary has already flown?

I wanted you to be happy, sweetheart. I wanted you to be in the colour supplements talking about your favourite restaurant (the Que Pasa) and the book you've most enjoyed reading this year (*The Scarsdale Diet Book*). I wanted you to have all the things I never had; rich fiancés, foreign travel, a Gucci bag. And what did I get? A 'phone call one day when I was serving up dinner.

'Oh Mam,' you said, 'it's me, Aveline. I'm in the Que Pasa, Mam. I'm having a meal with someone.'

As if you'd go to the Que Pasa for a manicure.

'He's a chap I know, Mam. He's very nice. I've known him for weeks now.'

But you had to telephone from the Que Pasa to tell us about it?

'His name's Oswald.'

Oswald. Funny how a name can grip at your heart and tear you in two. And rightly so. It was the beginning of a new chapter. She came running in that front door all breathless and dewy-eyed.

'Mam, Joey, I've got something to tell you. I'm engaged.'

Only a minute before she'd been having a meal with the fella – now this? It smacked of indecent haste. But before I could say anything, she lifted her hand to silence me.

'Listen, Mam – I want to tell you everything. He's thirty years old, his name is . . .'

'Oswald. We know that. It isn't the sort of name you forget.'

'I've known him for two months. He's kind, good and hard-working . . .'

Every word she said was like a drum roll at a beheading.

'He goes to church . . . every day – and . . . he's a vicar.'

A vicar? She'd only gone out and got herself engaged to a Proddy vicar!

God knows how it'll turn out. The engagement was so on and off that it was worse than the Bruno/Tyson match.

He knew, of course, Oswald, what a desperate mistake he'd made. He'd listened to his heart or some other part of his anatomy – but not to his head. When he simmered down and looked at her, he could see that our Aveline wasn't a natural choice for running the tombola stall at the vicarage fête. Even excepting the fact she'd been brought up as a daughter of the church of Rome she wasn't cut out to sit alone in a pew listening to him drearing on about Proddy duty and community work. A vicar's wife is a very special breed of person. It was all very well her rushing off to M & S and buying herself Tricel frocks and lambswool twin sets. But you can't hide who you are under a disguise; not for ever. And besides, I told her, it was the real Aveline that he'd fallen for; not some dowdy frump in man-made fibre.

Too late now, though. They're married, aren't they? And I will say she looked lovely at the wedding – but it wasn't what I'd hoped for her.

Is it ever? Maybe not.

Now all I can look forward to is a lot of little Proddy grandchildren – if Oswald can only manage to do it right.

DEAR FATHER, I PRAY MOST SINCERELY FOR MY DAUGHTER AVELINE WHO HAS GONE OVER TO THE OTHER SIDE AND MARRIED A PRODDY VICAR. SHE WANTS CHILDREN VERY BADLY, FATHER, SO IF YOU COULD HELP BY INCREASING OSWALD'S SPERM COUNT, SO THAT HE CAN MAKE HER PREGNANT QUICKLY, IT'LL PROBABLY BE BETTER IN THE LONG RUN. CHILDREN WILL GIVE HER AN OCCUPATION, FATHER. I CAN'T SEE HER SPENDING HER LIFE SITTING ON COMMITTEES AND DOING THE ALTAR FLOWERS. OUR AVELINE LOVES LITTLE ANIMALS, FATHER. THAT TIME SHE TOOK A JOB AS A VET'S RECEPTIONIST SHE WAS ALWAYS BRINGING HOME SICK VULTURES AND DISABLED HAMSTERS, BECAUSE SHE DIDN'T LIKE TO THINK OF THEM BEING ON THEIR OWN AT NIGHT. SO, DEAR FATHER, KNOWING HOW BUSY YOU GET, PERHAPS YOU COULD ASK ST FRANCIS TO KEEP AN EYE ON HER? SHE'S GOT A HEART OF GOLD AND SHE'D NEVER LET AN ANIMAL SUFFER. YOU SEE, SHE'S A GOOD GIRL, FATHER, AND SHE PROBABLY HAD NO IDEA HOW COLD IT'D BE, LIVING IN A PRODDY VICARAGE, WITH NO CENTRAL HEATING AND OSWALD IN BED BESIDE HER. SO, PLEASE, LOOK AFTER HER AND KEEP HER SAFE AND, IF THINGS GET REALLY BAD, WE COULD ALWAYS SAY THAT THE MARRIAGE HAD NEVER BEEN CONSUMMATED. BY THE LOOK OF OSWALD THAT WOULDN'T BE HARD TO BELIEVE. OH, AND THANK YOU FOR ALL THE LITTLE ANIMALS OF THIS WORLD, WHO DON'T KNOW THE DIFFERENCE BETWEEN CATHOLIC AND PRODDY AND LIVE IN THY SIGHT ALWAYS. AMEN.

Some Notes on Fashion

IT MAY BE of interest to some people if I tell you that all my sons wear black underpants. This may be seen as a fashionable statement or it may suggest that they are all devious – because I have heard it said that only devious men wear black underpants. (But the fact that it was Billy's Julie who passed this judgement could be more to do with their relationship than an actual considered observation.)

Everyone of them in black underpants.

Now, of course, you'd expect this from Joey, because he always wears everything black. But on the other hand you'd expect Adrian, who, when he's in an artistic mood can cram more colours into one garment than you'd get in a fruit salad, to go in for those little polka dot boxer shorts or a tasteful stripe; and Billy would certainly incline to those Y-fronts with obscene jokes and pictures on them if he had his way.

But, no. Every one of them wears black underpants. This is my sole contribution to the Boswell fashion catalogue for men. You could call it 'Fashion of Expediency'. If they're all black they can go in the same wash as the socks and this saves hours of sorting.

Apart from that, the boys go off and buy whatever they want with their own money. If they get something with a colour that runs, God help them. I haven't got time to do a random test and if an entire load comes out looking like a psychedelic nightmare, I can't help that. Washing is not my favourite occupation. I do it under sufferance – and I don't get paid.

An upturned litter bin

Maybe that was the original reason Joey took to black. It's a serviceable colour. It doesn't pick up and if it fades you can always call it grey and hand it on to Jack or our Billy.

Apart from Joey's all black leather outfits, the other boys usually wear jeans and a shirt and sweater, though Adrian had a suit when he was in Real Estate and Grandad has wardrobes full of stuff from around 1919 when he was first demobbed, right through to somewhere around 1973 when he last bought an outer garment.

My husband Freddie's clothes have nothing to do with me – or really anyone in the human race. He always manages to look as though he dressed in a hurry and shinned down the drainpipe even when I know for a fact that he's been sleeping on our sitting room sofa all night. He has the sort of clothes that would be impossible to go out and buy; the sort you see lying in mysterious heaps in lay-bys on motorways. Many's the time we've been driving along and I've thought – 'I'm sure that was our Freddie' – only to discover it was an over-turned litter bin or a discarded suitcase.

A free spirit with knickers on

What I'm trying to say is, there is no conformity in the dressing habits of the male Boswells – and although Aveline is a slave to fashion, it's a fashion of her own devising and I've never seen anyone else look even remotely like her. Which is both commendable for a model (you don't get two Twiggys, do you?) but is also confusing (I can never be absolutely certain when I see her out in the street, that she doesn't look a bit like a teenage version of her dad: a free spirit with knickers on).

My own clothes depend on how much change I get out of the supermarket bill or whether Joey gets a hand-out from the Ayatollah of the DHSS or the family insurance company. I mean things wear out, don't they? They have to be replaced. Most of my clothes used to 'get stolen off our washing line' and were replaced by the state – but half the neighbourhood got onto that one and ruined its credibility. There are some very greedy people about. They watch us like hawks. Every new idea our Joey dredges up from his brilliant mind goes into the public domain before the end of the month. He's working for people he doesn't even know – and without even so much as a thank you.

There are times when I put my foot down, of course. There are times when they must all look scrubbed and proper. I don't want my family confused with the riffraff that lives round here. Don't forget I am the one who suffered the humiliation of marrying a man whose trousers were held up with string. So, if it's a dress job – we go out and hire and Joey tries to claim back from the DHSS. On the grounds that a bus

One future queen,

one duchess......

conductor gets given a uniform and a policeman and even the girl in Sainsburys. Well then, why not us? When we go to a special function, we're representing the state. It's important to make a good impression, isn't it – if you're flying the flag for a democratic Britain.

Billy's marriage would have been a good occasion for us all to be seen at our best but, of course, we missed out on that, didn't we? We weren't invited, as you will soon discover.

So when it came to our Aveline's wedding I was determined that it should be the event of the season. I mean it wasn't at St Paul's and therefore wasn't a real wedding, being Proddy – but I didn't see any reason for us all to wear sackcloth and ashes. There are times when you have to make the best of a rotten job – and this was one of them.

All the men wore morning dress. (Funny, the English language, and very precise. Most men would agree that they should all go into mourning the minute they get wed. In mourning for their youth, for their days of 'hanky-panky', for all the women that they missed.) Well, as I say all the men wore morning dress. At least that's how it was meant to be, but Grandad changed at the last minute into his racing gear (as though he was going to a point-to-point and not to the wedding of his only granddaughter). He watched the groom's side of the church through binoculars and put a tenner each way on Oswald's mother in the three-thirty.

Aveline, of course, had very definite ideas about what she wanted to wear – most of which were totally unsuitable.

'You're getting married, Princess – it isn't a Pepsi-Cola advert,' I told her.

I thought she should look like Princess Diana – only we'd see that the frock had a good pressing before the big day. How they let that girl marry the future King of England in a frock that looked as though it'd just been slept in, I will never understand. But anyway, Aveline wasn't keen. She said she thought they'd skimped on the train and that she had in mind something altogether more sumptuous. I suggested that she

Aveline

...and our own princess

should save on the expense of the train and get new sitting room curtains for the vicarage instead, a Proddy vicar not exactly earning a fortune, but she was adamant. She gets very fixed ideas, does Aveline.

Then I suggested she should copy Sarah Ferguson. I mean she didn't have to have all that hair and if the frock was a bit on the blowsy side, that was more who was wearing it than the cut of the cloth. But, no – Aveline said she'd look like a gift-wrapped anorexic cabbage patch doll in a dress like that. The only answer would be to pad and she didn't fancy that in case it was a warm day and with her nerves she was bound to sweat. I knew what she meant – she had to walk down the aisle with her father and I dreaded to think what he'd look like. Actually not too bad, as things turned out. He has a certain style, I have to admit – but what I'll never forgive him for, was letting HER come to the church – Lilo Lil. She squeezed in beside Adrian and had every intention of ruining the whole ceremony. And it would have done – I was on the point of taking a swing at her – but the day was saved by the organist starting up 'Here Comes The Bride' – and there she was, our Aveline, with a train from here to eternity and a look on her face like a queen.

That's style for you. In the end she looked like Aveline Boswell and no one else –
and I'd take bets on who was the most beautiful princess in England that day.

Chapter Nine

Billy

I HADN'T REALISED that writing a book was going to be so like life. You know how there are things you keep putting off, like fixing dental appointments and defrosting the fridge? This chapter's been just like that. That's why I did that bit on Aveline's wedding dress – anything rather than tackle the untackleable. The north wall of the Eiger; the Pennine Way in a wheelbarrow; that's what the name BILLY suggests to me.

But he is my youngest – and he must be included.

I wonder if the biblical instruction 'go forth and multiply' is anything like washing a pair of Levis. Each time you do it, the jeans get weaker. Would that encapsulate what it's going to take me hours to describe? The genes getting weaker?

I don't know how you begin with Billy.

He was even born more or less by mistake – in fact you could almost see it as a miracle, considering his father spent more time cavorting round Sefton Park – in and out of the bushes, as he knew no shame – with a walloping great TART instead of being at home helping to bring up his family.

You could say Billy's conception was entirely her fault as well. You do some stupid things when you're patching up a quarrel and, of course, Freddie Boswell has never been known to have a serious conversation when a bit of 'hanky-panky' would do as well.

So, there I was with another baby. I began to think I'd been chosen to found a dynasty, or a football club; the Boswell Wanderers or Boswell Athletics, anything but Boswell United, thanks to her; thanks to Madam with the over-active glands; great big gallumphing Lilo Lil – the TART.

Well, as I say, the Lord blessed our union yet again; though he must've been quick. By the time Lilo Lil was on the scene Freddie's energy was at a premium. If he so much as sneezed I was in danger of ending up pregnant.

Of all my children Billy is the one you could say is the product of a single parent family. If only Joey had been a bit older and more on the ball at the time I could have

Billy

claimed single parent benefit.

Not that Freddie and I were divorced, of course. You can't to that in the real church, and anyway, I'll be damned before I'll let her prance about with a legal status; once a TART always a TART; I shall see to that.

Billy grew rapidly. It was as though he was in some terrible hurry. He was – but I didn't know then why. He thrashed his way through school, telling the teachers better ways of doing things and re-writing every subject that came his way. *The William Boswell History of England* should be required reading. He actually managed to get minus marks in his mock O Level. Minus? I queried it at the PTA meeting and a patient young man explained that not only had he not bothered to answer a single question on the exam sheet, but he'd written an essay on the girls in his form instead. Well, not exactly an essay – more a list really; a score card. He just rated them all out of ten.

He knew it all, did Billy. There wasn't a thing his elder brothers had done that he hadn't done before, more of, and for a greater reward. Well, of course, you switch off after a while, don't you? You cease to listen and in no time at all, or actually when he was sixteen, he wandered over the road one day to No 41 for a bit of attention and was gob-smacked in love with Julie Jefferson by the time he reeled back again.

Julie

Well, it wasn't good news. But then is it ever, where the heart is concerned? I mean, I thought she was a nice enough kid. She hadn't got Aveline's flair, but then few of them have; and if I'd been her mother I'd have got her to do something with her hair. But I was prejudiced, not against her as I say, but you are what your family is and Julie's family left a lot to be desired. Her dad is away at sea and her mam is away at the pub. That more or less sums it up. Of course, from Billy's point of view it was ideal; nice little love nest all to themselves and handy for home when he was hungry. What could be better? If ever Mrs Jefferson did catch them there together, she was beyond caring. She was always pissed. It was her vocation, I think. That and a high contralto voice. She's the only woman I know who can sing Nellie Dean in four different languages – which doesn't make her an intellectual, just very friendly with the foreign sailors.

Now, up until this point Billy was following in the well-trodden path of his brothers. But he found a little side track and decided to go up that instead.

He was at the time working as a one-man-band. No, I am not speaking metaphorically. Our Billy came up with the dizzying scheme of strapping cymbals to his knees and sticking a mouth organ in his gob and going out into the wide world expecting people to hand over good money to hear his rendition of *It's Been A Hard Day's Night* and *Puppet On A String*. I had to be prevented from paying him just to take the cymbals off – they make a terrible racket in the house – and Mongy nearly left home when he practised the mouth organ. I think it must've reminded him of his wolf ancestors and given him the urge to roam free. But, whatever we may each've privately thought, you had to hand it to him that it was a novel way of helping to fill the family pot. Well, of course, actually it didn't help fill the family pot much – because all those unsuspecting people out there felt much the same as we did about it: reasonable idea, but terrible noise.

And then Julie dropped her little, well-timed bombshell. She was pregnant. Billy was gob-smacked. He could not figure it. It didn't seem possible. How could it happen to him? He wasn't ready for it. He was only a teenager. Maybe it was somebody else's baby?

There were times when my sympathies were entirely with Julie – in the early days. But then she must have known what she was taking on. You only have to look at Billy to hear the four minute warning. And maybe in the end we all get what we deserve – though how I deserved Freddie Boswell is a mystery and what Aveline did to be lumbered with Oswald Carter is beyond comprehension. But Julie – she gave as good as she got, and more.

'I'm making this baby, not you Billy,' she'd tell him, when not a moment before it'd been all his fault. 'It's in my body. I'm feeding it, building it, I'm giving birth to it. All you did, Billy Boswell, was fumble your way through some biological frenzy.'

Biological frenzy? She made it sound like a washing powder. She could be very cruel and cutting. And she certainly had a field day over being pregnant. She wouldn't accept any help from me; would do it her way. She had a case packed and by the front door for the last month before it was due.

'It isn't due for a month yet,' we'd reassure Billy.

'I know that,' he'd snap, all pent-up emotion and paternal anxiety. 'I keep telling her that, don't I? "What do you know about it?" she says. "Well, I know a pregnancy

Billy

lasts nine months," I tell her. "So where were you on Monday, the 25th of January between ten o'clock and the rest of the night?" she said. "What's that got to do with it?" I said. "You see," she said, "you think you know everything about the game of life, Billy, and you can't even remember the kick-off!"'

Poor lad, he was like putty in her hands. She rolled him and moulded him and muddled him up till he didn't know what had hit him. And, I wouldn't care, but it was us that had to suffer the damaged goods. Every time they had words he'd hot foot it across the road and subject us to all the gory details. We've had Billy's head hitting the table and the tears flowing more times than the Liberals have lost their deposit.

And she has a will of steel. She will not bend. Once Julie makes up her mind it becomes an instant, immovable law. Of course she didn't like us from the start, that was the trouble. But then, if she didn't like us, why did she encourage 'hanky-panky' with one of us? She must've known that we stand as one when there's trouble. If you have a relationship with one Boswell you're expected at least to be civil to the rest. But not Miss Julie at No 41.

Love birds?

The first time she and I crossed swords was over the birth of the baby. I wasn't going to have my first grandchild come into the world in a public ward at Mill Road Maternity. You never know who's been in the bed before you there – you can't even be sure of the sheets. I mean they say they wash them – but do they properly boil them? No, I was determined on Sandfield Park Nursing Home and that's where we booked her in. She only went and told the ambulance men there'd been a mistake and to take her to Mill Road, didn't she? It took all Joey's charm and a personal escort of Boswells to see she ended up in the right place.

Billy attended the birth. He said it was a miracle. Quite unlike any other confinement. He certainly gave us a shove by shove account – enough to put you off the whole natural world. Well, it was his first baby, wasn't it? It was bound to be unique.

It was a little girl, actually. I was sure Billy would father a boy. But then Julie didn't let him have any say in that either.

So now we have a seventeen-year-old unmarried father in our midst. Then his troubles really started. (It all happens in our family. I'm sometimes frightened to open my eyes in the morning in case the house has gone off somewhere in the night.)

Next thing we know, Billy gets a letter from Julie. A letter? She only lives across the street; she could have leaned out the window and called. But no:

> Dear Billy,
>   I have been worried lately – about us living here – about the future of our baby – about the world. I know you try hard – but is busking the right job for the father of my child, Billy? I'm sorry, something in me can't wait any longer for you to get the big break and to be clashing your cymbals on the tele. I don't see it happening somehow. I told you about my friends in London. Well, I've gone down to see what its like. Perhaps the streets are paved with hope. I'll phone you when I'm settled.
>   Don't worry about the baby.
>
>   Love Julie

Well, of course, Billy was beside himself. It was like two of him sitting at our table, both ranting and raving at the same time.

'She has no right. I'm the father of that baby. She's kidnapped my child . . .'

God bless and save us, it was like the big film.

Poor Billy. He wasn't 'ready for this' either and I must admit I felt a bit responsible. Julie hadn't just run away from him; she'd run away from all of us. Me, particularly. I think in a way she's afraid of me; she sees me as too powerful. She once told Billy she thought I thought I was personally related to God. I can't help it if I *know* what's right; it certainly doesn't mean I always manage to do it. But that's why she'd gone – and maybe she needed time to think. Anyway, something must have decided her that she could do worse than our Billy, because she came back. Maybe she realised that living free in No 41, even putting up with Billy, was better than trying to make ends meet in London – everything's astronomical down there. Funny how economics governs even your sex life.

Billy – the tycoon

Billy, in a desperate attempt to prove himself and to appear mature, and encouraged by Joey, gave up his busking and, with a grant from the Enterprise Allowance Scheme he started out doing his own sandwich round. Apparently he'd always had an interest in food, which I hadn't realised. The way he grabs anything that's put in front of him and crams it into his gob reminds me of Mongy.

The relief of being shot of the cymbals was tarnished a little by having bottled mayonnaise stuck to the ceiling, when he shook the bottle with the top off, and tinned tuna fish flying through the air each morning, as he tried to butter fifty rounds and fill them with mouth-watering combinations in five minutes, having failed to be woken by four alarms, two radios and the steady tramp of brothers through the bedroom.

SAN FRANCISCO

That, of course, was if he was sleeping at home. What usually seemed to happen was that he started off over at No 41 for the evening; he'd get a bit amorous after *Sportsnight*; she'd give in; they'd just be getting settled, then they'd have a row and he'd come banging back over here sobbing and sighing. There should be a groove in the road, running in a diagonal from the Jeffersons' house to ours; that's when he was walking it, of course. After he had his car he used to drive across. He's the only lad I know who regularly reversed all the way home! Well, it saved him the effort of using several gears and actually having to turn the wheel.

The rows seemed to be getting more frequent and we tried to help as best we could. I thought I'd do a bit of a party for the baby's christening – a cake, nothing elaborate, just a way of marking a once-in-a-lifetime event. But Julie didn't want a party, Billy told me, she wanted it:

'. . . quiet and dignified. She doesn't want any fuss.'

We weren't going to make any fuss – just the family, that's all. Our family and her family.

'She hasn't got a family,' Billy said.

Well, she'd got a mother and father, and a brother somewhere.

'Her dad's at sea – her mam – well, you know, her mam's all over the place. They're not like us, Mam,' Billy said.

THE COLLECTOR ™

This is the Golden Gate Bridge. It's nice here. You should come over. You could help me make the sandwiches. They have names like 'A Leg Over on Rye' and 'A pink Triangle with Mustard Relish' (thats ham and Pumpernickle for gays). Give my love to Mam and don't let Julie get you down, kid

Stay cool
Jack

63c

Billy Boswell

30 Kelsall Street

Liverpool

UK

©1987 SAN FRANCISCO NOVELTIES 1850 UNION ST #494 SF . CALIF 94123

He can be very sensitive – once every twelve years or so. He made me feel quite sorry for poor little Julie, the little soul. But, of course, I should have waited before I wasted any compassion.

'And the other thing is,' Billy continued. Have you ever noticed that whenever there's 'another thing' it's never good? 'I've been putting off telling you this, Mam, but the christening isn't at St Paul's. It's at St Mary's.'

I couldn't get it for a minute. He seemed to be speaking in a foreign language. St Mary's? St Mary's is a Protestant church.

'It's how she wants it, Mam.'

Then it sank in. Oh, my God. My grandchild – brought up a Proddy? (This was in the days, of course, before Aveline married her vicar. I'm used to being under siege now. But then it was all new and painful.)

'I don't see what difference it makes,' Billy says, 'church is a church. God is God.'

'Wash your mouth out, Billy Boswell.'

'Unless there are two Gods?'

'There is only one God, Billy. I don't know who they pray to.'

'Oh come on, Mam,' he says, 'we all speak to the same fella.'

He didn't care at all that his daughter would be brought up one of them. Everything I'd taught him had been in vain.

Francesca's christening – if you can call it that in a Proddy church.

'Don't you see – she won't go to confession, she won't go to mass, she won't know the meaning of love, and unity, and human understanding.'

I couldn't get through to him. He just sat there munching scones.

'My God, Billy,' I yelled, 'Father Dooley will never forgive us. He'll do his holy nut!'

Francesca, they called her in the sight of the Proddy God, but I realised that, wherever you are – even be it a Proddy church, God watches over you and listens and so I just offered up an apology to him – after all, the little mite can change her mind later and come over to us. It's only a temporary arrangement.

During the ceremony, when we were all standing round the font – plain church, not much in the way of decoration, smelling of Vim and Brasso – the cordless 'phone rang in Aveline's bag. The vicar carried on as if nothing had happened. It was a call for Adrian. He'd got a job. Not, as it turned out, a suitable job – but nevertheless it does go to bear out the usefulness of the machine. No matter where you are, you're still in touch with the world. And, to give the vicar his due, he ended the ceremony blessing the baby and congratulating Adrian, which was, I thought, civil of him.

So now we've got a seventeen-year-old, unmarried father with a daughter christened Francesca. Billy's life continued like one of those endless soap operas being shown out of sequence. The next big event in his life should have happened much earlier on. Really it'd have been better if it hadn't happened at all. In fact, in some ways, I wonder if it ever did. None of us were there. We, the family – I never thought

Billy wouldn't be part of that – we were looking after altogether more pressing matters; we were all putting on a brave face at the trial – yes, I said 'trial' – of my husband, his father. Billy's own father standing trial for theft of a municipal muck cart (this is another story and belongs in another place), and Billy wasn't there. And where was he? Sneaking off with Julie Jefferson to some registry office to get married, with Francesca in their arms and Julie's brother as best man.

'It's how Julie wanted it, Mam' is all he says in his defence.

'How Julie wanted it? That's all you ever say. Haven't you got a mind, Billy? Don't you have any opinions? Does she write, play *and* conduct the music of your life? Haven't you got a GOB?'

'Our Dad needed support today,' Aveline chimes in, 'he needed all of us.'

'It was an accident,' Billy whines, 'the date I mean – it wasn't planned. We had to take the date the registrar gave us.'

The wedding – to which we weren't invited.

'The registrar! Oh my God. No mass. No white frock. No carnations . . .'

'And no ham salad!' Billy yells, standing to attention. 'She didn't want a ham salad wedding.'

'We could have talked, Billy,' Joey tells him. 'We could have played it any way you wanted.'

'We did it the way we wanted.'

That boy's learning stubbornness from his . . . from Julie.

'You didn't take Mam's feeling into consideration though, did you?' Joey can be chilling when he's quiet and calm. Thank God for Joey. 'A wedding's a big thing in life, Billy. It's a time for family. You let us down.'

Someone had to say it.

'Don't say those words. I don't like those words.'

We'll have tears soon.

'So, when you decided to spend nights over the road,' I told him, 'we all supported you and ignored the neighbours. When she became pregnant we stood by you and ignored the neighbours. When you had her christened in a Protestant church we went through that pathetic service, and ignored the neighbours. And now – we come home from the court, where your father has been fighting for his life, and we find that you've sneaked off, got married and ignored *us*. You're not a son of mine, Billy.'

I couldn't help it. I was that choked.

And what did he do? He wanted to know if he could have his dinner!

'You have your dinner with your wife from now on,' Joey told him.

That was the same day that Eddie arrived to stay. A criminal husband, a banished son, and a gay relative knocking at the door. Life can be very hard.

And now, of course, they're getting divorced. Well, you could see it coming, couldn't you?

It's all solicitors and splitting the belongings now. And little Francesca? I can see a tug of love coming up next with the neighbours hanging out of the windows watching every move.

He's not ready for all this, our Billy. Poor lad, he was bound to crack under the strain.

'All these things that are happening between you and me are turning me into a bad person, Julie,' he said. 'I wish I'd never met you now, you've made me suspicious of women, you've made me afraid of marriage. you've made me hate ginger sponge pudding and you've made me want to kill your solicitor . . .'

He could see himself turned into a murderer. But that wasn't the real Billy.

He's the one who stopped the rush hour traffic to rescue a pigeon that had been hit by a truck. Caused a traffic jam a mile long. I was proud of him then.

He brought the bird home and he persuaded Grandad to keep it – which must've taken some doing. Grandad can't stand lodgers in the house. Only he couldn't bring it in here, because birds give me asthma. He called it Prescott – because that was the name of the street where he rescued it. It had a broken wing – I expect Adrian would see symbolism in that. Our Billy had a broken wing himself by then; that's what Adrian would say.

He's always been in such a rush at life. No wonder he collapsed and went under. Nervous exhaustion, that's what the doctor said. But then, is there any wonder? He

Billy

Billy. It looks as if he's just got up – but he often looks like that.

packed into a year what most men settle for in a lifetime. Conception, birth, christening, marriage and divorce. He will rush things.

He once helped a little old lady home with some plants and ended up planting them for her. Five minutes after she told him that her rockery had never looked so lovely, he came home with 'Billy's Nurseries' written on the side of his van.

If it wasn't an old lady – it was a pigeon.

'It just sat there,' he told Joey. 'Nobody stopped, it just sat there. It was frightened. I know how that feels.'

'Well, being frightened comes natural to a pigeon, it's permanently frightened . . .'

But Billy wouldn't be consoled.

'I thought to myself "If it was me lying in the road, someone would have called an ambulance . . ."'

'They don't call ambulances for pigeons, Billy.'

'Because they don't care. That's why. They don't care.'

I've just realised, Billy does care – but he rushes so fast you don't always notice it.

DEAR FATHER, YOU PROBABLY KNOW WHAT TO MAKE OF MY BILLY. I EXPECT YOU UNDERSTAND EVERYTHING THERE IS TO ABOUT HIM – THOUGH IT MUST TAX EVEN YOU. I THINK HE MEANS WELL, FATHER. IT'S JUST THAT HE DOESN'T STOP TO THINK FIRST. IT'S NO USE MY ASKING YOU TO INTERCEDE FOR HIM, BECAUSE HE'S ALWAYS WAY AHEAD OF ME. FATHER, HE DOESN'T WANT A DIVORCE, IT'S HER – JULIE – AND SHE ISN'T A CATHOLIC, SO I WONDER IF IT REALLY WILL COUNT. I MEAN, I'M NOT TRYING TO BARGAIN WITH YOU OR BAMBOOZLE YOU, BUT FATHER, IF YOU COULD SEE A WAY TO LETTING BILLY HAVE A FRESH START HE MIGHT HAVE LEARNT SOMETHING FROM ALL HIS MISTAKES. EXCEPT EVEN AS I WRITE THIS I REALISE HE WON'T HAVE. OH FATHER, YOU'LL HAVE TO SORT HIM OUT, I CAN'T. HE'S TOO CONFUSING. THY WILL BE DONE AND IF EVER YOU HAVE TIME TO EXPLAIN WHY IT'S BEING DONE IN THE WAY IT'S DONE, I'D BE MORE THAN GRATEFUL. BLESS LITTLE FRANCESCA AND FORGIVE HER MOTHER. AND A SPECIAL PRAYER FOR PRESCOTT WHO DIDN'T SURVIVE AT GRANDAD'S, BUT AT LEAST THE POOR CREATURE DIED IN LOVE – THANKS TO BILLY. AMEN.

A Visitor

WE'RE NOT GIVEN to swanking in our family. Probably people'd think that we don't have much to swank about. If your entire household is on social security and you have a husband/father who spends half his time with a TART and the other half pushing a cart round the streets, you'd hardly want to go around advertising the fact.

But I have five good children: a published poet, a seasoned traveller, a self-employed father of one, a one-time model and an Adonis, and sometimes, when they're all gathered round the dinner table and we're about to say our prayers, I look at them and I think it was worth all the sweating and heaving and shoving and straining that I had to go through to bring them into this world.

If that's swanking, then I'm a swank. And if I'm a swank, I may as well go for broke and mention that I once had Linda McCartney in my kitchen. The neighbours are still talking about it. I just walk by and bask in their envy. It's a lovely sensation. The most any of them can boast about is a Blue Peter badge or a day trip to Windermere.

It happened that Linda McCartney was being interviewed on Radio Merseyside and Joey, never one to pass up a trick, tipped Billy off that there'd be bound to be a crowd at the door and if they'd been hanging around for some time, they'd be glad of a sandwich to munch on and he should get himself down there and supply the demand. So off he went and, being a friendly soul, he not only sold a lot of egg and cress, cheese and pickle and some tuna and cucumber (which are always less popular on account of the fact that he cuts the cucumber thick enough to sole shoes) but he also got talking to the celebrity herself, while she was signing people's autographs.

God knows what possessed him, but he found himself saying:

'If you'd like to come to tea in our house, my Mam makes smashing cakes . . .' Which happens to be true – but does smack of swanking.

Well, of course, I don't suppose he thought for one minute that she'd take him up on the offer – and knowing Billy, I expect he forgot he'd even said it a moment later. So I was all alone in the house when this great, big, blue Mercedes taxi pulled up outside. That made the curtains twitch along the street, I can tell you.

Linda had only taken him up on the invitation, hadn't she? And where was Billy? Out, of course. That's so typical. Our Billy is *always* 'out'. How he managed to father a child is a mystery. I've never known him see any job through to the end.

Me – when I'm not writing.

103

My friend Linda

Billy

So, as I say, I entertained Linda McCartney. To tell you the truth, I didn't know who she was at the time. But I must say she was a very nice lady. No side to her. A vegetarian so she'd have got on well with Joey. From America, so I thought she might have met our Jack. Of course, she pointed out that it's a big place – but she'd have recognised him at once: black hair, dark, dark eyes and a sad, Social Security face; that's my Jack – or it was before he started working with a lot of gays. God knows what he looks like now. The photos he sent were a bit blurred but I thought he looked suspiciously brown. I know Joey says it'd be natural sun tan, but I just wish he'd come home; too much sun is bad for you and if it's pancake I'll personally paralyse him.

Anyway she said she'd called to see Billy and I said she'd best come in and wait for him. Funny how you can talk to some people; tell them things that are difficult to say to those who're really close to you.

I told her about Lilo Lil and she understood, did Linda. She said her chest sounded like a lot of competition.

'I've worked all these years for that man and those children, Linda,' I told her. 'They've never come home to an empty house or a bare table – never. No matter what goes on in the world outside – in here is home . . .'

I'm sorry. It sounds a bit moaning but, well . . . it hurts sometimes. Anyway, she understood me.

'Sure it hurts – everything hurts – we come into this world crying and we go out that way.' That's what she said to me, and you could tell she knew. 'Sometimes I think God was a woman-hater,' she said. 'Why else would he have lumbered us with men?'

I'm not sure I was the best one to answer that, considering I'd brought another four of them into this world.

'I wonder if there's an after life?' I said to her.

Well, how often d'you get to talk like that – unless you're on your knees in a confession box?

'God, I hope not,' she said. 'I can't wait to get my feet up.'

I mean – all the traumas we go through, all the emotions, the anguish. What's it for? That's what I wanted to know. That's what I said to this stranger, sitting in my kitchen, eating my cakes. Why do we go through it? Everything God did has a pattern. This helps this, this couldn't survive without this, this and this makes this, and finally we have this. But – what? What is it that we *do* have . . . finally?

'Nothing,' Linda said. 'We have nothing.'

'Not much of a reward, is it?'

'Maybe that's the best he could come up with – a permanent state of nothing,' she said.

'I don't know why I worry about these things,' I said. 'Do you – do you worry about things, Linda?'

She smiled then.

'Me?' she said. 'I worry about everything. Kids, dogs, trees, other people's people. Once I accidentally trod on a snail – I didn't kill it, but I couldn't sleep all night for worrying about how it felt, sitting there without a shell. Mind you,' she said, 'we're all sitting here without our shells, aren't we?'

And I could see what she meant. But then I thought, there's the family.

'Family is strength, I always say,' I told her.

Mrs Boswell's Slice of Bread

And that's what I've been trying to explain in this book.

The family. The children. My father. And, finally, I suppose even my husband. Yes, in the end, I'll have to write about Freddie as well.

Family. The reason for it all.

When she left, my friend Linda, I was appalled to discover she'd kept her taxi standing by; and there I'd been nattering away about life and God and all the other mysteries.

It must have cost her a fortune. But she said she didn't mind. She said she'd enjoyed her visit and she was sorry she'd missed Billy. She was so natural. Just like one of us. She has a husband in work, mind, so she doesn't have to worry too much at present.

I'll tell you what though – her taxi driver reminded me of someone. But I've never been able to place him.

Linda's taxi driver. I'm sure I know that face.

Chapter Ten

Grandad

My father, Grandad to us all, has been on this earth for 75 years. When he was a lad, it was all fields and farms round here. They'd never heard words like nuclear, radio-active, insecticide, pollution. You could go out into the streets and drink the puddles in those days.

It must be like a different world for him now; a different planet. Here he is living in the same house he's always lived in – well, virtually, there's been the odd little move for poverty's sake but apart from that he has been here – like a camera with its shutter open, watching the changing scene.

Grandad – a typical smile

He's outlived two world wars, the depression, Macmillan's never-had-it-so-good era and Harold Wilson's let's-all-do-it-together-in-a-Gannex-mac years. He's witnessed the swinging sixties, the silly seventies and the you're-paying-for-it-now eighties. He's seen unemployment soar and the environment suffer. He's seen me marry and he's seen Lilo Lil elbow me out of the way. He's watched his five grandchildren grow up, more or less – some more, some less. He's had a gay to stay and a discharged criminal as a lodger. Through all this he has remained steadfast to his own nature; bossy and opinionated, the true head of our family.

In fact, Grandad represents the family in microcosm; he's like all my kids and my husband and every other man I have ever met all rolled into one. He's selfish and self-centred and concerned and very annoying and I sometimes wake up at night, terrified that he's died all alone next door and that I wasn't there to help him, reassure him and hold his hand. Mind, he's tough, of course, but when you reach that sort of age you can't help wondering how the end will happen. Will he be asleep in bed, or sitting in his chair, or standing in the road waving his stick? Or maybe he'll be right in the middle of a Danish pastry. Or putting the world to rights. Maybe he'll just stop, in mid sentence – and that'll be it.

When he goes the centre of our family will go. We won't be for ever rushing round with a tray of food or a mug of tea. There'll be no one for each of us to turn to when things get us down. The wonderful thing about Grandad is that no matter what you tell him, he stays the same. You can't shock him. He's heard it all before. Just when you think you've gone too far, his one-track mind is off thinking about the next meal or the danger of modern living or remembering the good times when the world was clean and he had the vigour to fulfil the cravings that still haunt him.

It must be really terrible to be old in years – yet young inside. He said once that he felt like a toy that's been put back in its box. He said his winder was stuck – all it needed was a touch and off he'd go. But that nobody opened the box any more.

'I'm useless,' he said, 'old and useless. There was a time I could put my hand in my wallet and say – there you go, lad, there you go. But now . . . I'm just a parasite.'

If he only knew. The contribution he makes to the family is beyond reckoning.

We claim our rent to him; he claims his to us. There's his incontinence money, his hearing aid money, the gardening equipment allowance – well, that is legitimate, he does have window boxes. When he started drinking a lot of water and Dr Bennet said he'd have to be tested for diabetes, Joey went straight down and claimed for a fridge to keep the insulin in – just in case it came to that.

The elderly are a special case, and Grandad is the most special of them all. There's nothing that he might need that we haven't claimed for. If he went, we'd be practically bankrupt.

Mind, his moods can change very fast. One minute he's in despair because he's a parasite; the next he's putting our rent up. All we could do was put his up in retaliation, thereby balancing the status quo. Caring for the elderly is a constant tug of war between discipline and indulgence; it's like having a puppy in the house, or a baby. You can't let up for a minute. If they think they've got the upper hand you're done for.

The thing is, he spends too much time sitting and thinking. He gets bored and when he gets bored he gets fretful. Once he's fretful there's no knowing what he'll get up to.

Sitting, getting fretful – and about to be clamped!

Grandad and Joey

Like, one day he wouldn't have any lemon pie. He loves my lemon pie. But he wouldn't eat it. He said the government had banned using some chemical because it was poisonous, but they hadn't banned making it, so we sell it to the Mexicans, and they spray their lemons with it and then they sell their lemons back to us and we eat them and consequently the banned poison. So, no thank you, he didn't want any more of my lemon pie; he'd have treacle tart instead. Or, another time, he went off honey – because the bees are radioactive.

If he suspects the eggs aren't free range – he ejects them through the letter box. Well, you can't always be sure, can you? I say to him, sometimes, that the hens that lay them do at least run round the hut a lot. But of course that isn't good enough for Grandad.

He went through a bad patch when he couldn't keep his legs still in bed at night. He was wearing holes in the sheets. I had to get the doctor, who gave him something to relax his legs. No time at all he was complaining that his arms were waving about – like an octopus, he said he was, just like he'd seen on a Wildlife programme on the tele.

He will read his medical book. I tell him it's full of bad news.

'You'd have to be a doctor to understand all this stuff, Grandad,' I say. 'Lower backache, swelling of the ankles and sometimes the hands. Breathlessness, the inability to sleep and physical restlessness . . .'

'I've got all those symptoms,' he told me. 'Jumping about, I am, like a fish on a slab . . .'

But if he'd only bothered to read to the end of the page he'd have discovered that he was about to plunge into labour. I mean, if he's going to give birth I need a bit of warning – and so does Joey; there are forms to fill in and story-rights to sell.

But then the point is – we none of us know what we're going to be like when it comes to us, do we? We think we'll be all right and still have all our marbles, but you can't be sure can you? It could be that one day we'll be wondering how it happened that we've ended up cantakerous and frail and lonely.

I see him sitting waiting for me sometimes, when he doesn't know I'm there. A little old man, with a shock of hair and a vile temper; leaning on his stick, cursing at life. All day, just waiting for me to return from the supermarket or wherever I've had the nerve to go. As if I'm his personal servant. Which in a way I am, I suppose, because we do draw an attendance allowance, of course. But that's how he spends his days; just waiting. Waiting for his breakfast, waiting for his lunch, waiting for his tea. Like the stations of the cross; the pit-stops of life.

Joey once took him to task about it.

'Maybe you ought to try thinking about something else, Grandad, instead of your stomach.'

'What else is there to think about?' he demanded. 'My hands are shaky, my eyes are half-blind, my heart is wonky, my legs are knackered – and all my other bits have gone into premature retirement.'

Joey was at a loss for a minute. They have a way of undermining you, the elderly; a way of making you see only their narrow horizon.

'Well,' he said, I think, a bit desperately, considering what he then offered; '. . . think about love, Grandad.'

Love? Grandad?

'Love!' he exclaimed, revelling in the scorn. 'D'you want my brain to go an' all? I thought about love once – and I ended up with your Grannie. She went up that aisle like a bulldog with a bone in its mouth – and she never let go of me again until she was taking her last breath. God bless her! She was some woman. I bet you any money she's up there now, bossing the Almighty himself about. Telling him when to make it rain, when to make it shine – and woe betide him if he leaves the lavatory seat up.'

Personally, most of my actual conversations with Grandad are over the 'phone. Well, I don't have time to go running in at all hours, but at least with the telephone you can keep in touch.

—— A PASSING THOUGHT ——

We should try and get British Telecom to sponsor this book. After all, I'm giving them a lot of free publicity and they make a fortune out of us each quarter.

You're never alone with a phone

A conversation with Grandad can go something like this:

Me: Hello, Grandad?

Him: Who's that?

Me: You know very well.

Him: I do not. It could be any of a number of women. When's my dinner coming?

Me: I'm running a bit late – any minute now.

Him: What is it?

Me: Roast potatoes, cheese pie and broccoli – all right?

Him: I don't like broccoli.

Me: Roast potatoes and cheese pie?

Him: I'm sick of cheese pie.

Me: A lot of roast potatoes then.

I admit it isn't exactly a conversation – but it takes two to talk and he isn't exactly animated. But that's where he thinks we fail him.

'Nobody talks to me,' he once said. That was when he said he'd fallen one time and we all went rushing round – only to find there was nothing wrong with him at all. He just wanted attention, I suppose.

'What d'you mean – nobody talks to you?' I said. 'We're always bringing you trays. We ring you. You ring us.'

'Nobody tells me anything,' he said. 'It's just words, not sentences.'

I knew at once what he meant.

'You just fob me off with trivialities,' he said. 'It's not conversation. All I get is "All right Grandad?" "How's it going Grandad?" "Hello Grandad." "Tarra Grandad." Occasionally, if I'm really lucky, one of you'll say – "It's a nasty day, Grandad!" Well, I don't need that, do I? I can see for myself if it's pissing down, can't I?'

Certain things, of course, we try to keep from him – on account of his age. Well, most things really; only we don't seem to succeed. He must have one of the finest pairs of ears that the good Lord ever made. Which is just as well, for as long as they last, because it means we can use his deaf aid money on other more urgent needs until such time as it's needed for its legitimate purpose.

When Aveline was rushed to hospital with her anaemia – well, I mean, we didn't know at the time what it was but it turned out to be anaemia – Grandad was sitting outside the house. (He uses the street as a garden in summer; and why not? He fought in two world wars for this land.)

'You'd better go in, Grandad,' Joey told him – not wanting him to see the ambulance and be worried.

'I don't want to,' he said. 'Why should I?' he said. 'Piss off,' he said.

Well, you learn to play people at their own games, don't you?

'All right, Grandad, you stay put. Only they're coming along, spraying the street.'

That moved him. Well no, to be honest, Jack and Joey moved him. They just picked him up, chair and all and carried him inside. But he was willing to go.

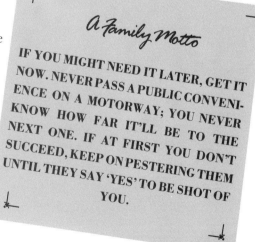

A Family Motto

IF YOU MIGHT NEED IT LATER, GET IT NOW. NEVER PASS A PUBLIC CONVENIENCE ON A MOTORWAY; YOU NEVER KNOW HOW FAR IT'LL BE TO THE NEXT ONE. IF AT FIRST YOU DON'T SUCCEED, KEEP ON PESTERING THEM UNTIL THEY SAY 'YES' TO BE SHOT OF YOU.

'Spraying the streets now, are they? They've killed everything, so they're killing us now.'

All we can do, as far as I can see it, is keep him with us and try to make him feel wanted and avoid getting into too many arguments with him. Because otherwise, to be honest, you sometimes feel like giving him a shove towards his maker – he can be so infuriating. Then just when you think you can't stand him another minute he'll remind you of how even he was once a young man:

'Days of hormones and adrenalin. Days of being brave. You just opened your mouth in them days and said what your body thought.'

And you find yourself thinking, 'Oh, Grandad . . .'

Mrs Boswell's Slice of Bread

Grandad - with what looks like a halo - but it CAN'T be!

DEAR FATHER, BLESS AND KEEP MY DAD, UNTIL HIS TIME IS READY TO COME TO YOU, AND MY MOTHER, WHO MUST BE HEARTILY SICK OF WAITING FOR HIM. SHE WAITED FOR HIM OFTEN ENOUGH IN HER LIFETIME BUT THIS LAST STINT MUST HAVE DRIVEN HER CRAZY. I HOPE IT ISN'T TRUE THAT ONCE YOU'RE DEAD YOU KNOW ALL THAT HAPPENED DURING YOUR LIFE, BECAUSE REALLY, FATHER, IT'D BE MUCH BETTER IF MOTHER DIDN'T KNOW ABOUT GRANDAD AND EDIE MATHESON AND THE TIME THEY SPENT AT THE HOTEL FLAMINIO, IN ROME – OH, A LONG TIME AGO. HE WAS ON A BUSINESS TRIP, AND SHE GOT HER FROCK CAUGHT IN HIS OVERNIGHT CASE AND HE SAID TO HER, 'I MARRIED THE LAST ONE IT CAUGHT.' FORGIVE AN OLD MAN, FATHER, IF HE REMEMBERS THE MURKIER FRAGMENTS OF HIS PAST. THANK YOU, DEAR FATHER, FOR KEEPING HIM HEALTHY MOST OF THE TIME AND, WHEN HE'S NOT, THANK YOU FOR WATCHING OVER HIM. OH, AND BLESS HIS CANARY, ROSE, WHO GOT EGG-BOUND ONCE TOO OFTEN AND PASSED ON. IF MOTHER IS LOOKING AFTER HER UP THERE, AT LEAST I KNOW HER CAGE'LL BE CLEAN. GRANDAD NEVER GOT ROUND TO MUCKING HER OUT. SHE COULD HAVE DIED FROM HER OWN SALMONELLA THE STATE SHE WAS IN DOWN HERE. MAY SHE REST IN PEACE. AMEN.

Chapter Eleven

Shifty & Celia Higgins

IT'S AN ODD fact that has been noted before that the darkest clouds have a silver lining. Mind, the sun has to be shining somewhere for this phenomenon to occur and quite frankly if Shifty is about he's more than likely to have nicked it and so we'd all be in total darkness anyway. But, if I have got to waste good time writing a few words about our *distant* cousin – who has managed to get his feet lodged under my table for a surprisingly long time – then it's worth my remembering that it is only him looking for sanctuary under our roof that brought Celia Higgins to the street and I have enjoyed her company in much the same way that I enjoyed the visit from my friend, Linda. A woman needs a female friend. It can't be all men, or you'd end up screaming. And Celia has been a good friend to me – because she understands men.

> *A Motto of Celia's*
>
> **MEN HAVE THEIR DANGLY BITS AND WOMEN HAVE THEIR CONSCIENCE.**

Shifty's antecedents would fill three pages of the Domesday Book. His mother was Freddie's sister, Aida. They were a stuck-up lot, the Boswells. Aida? They got the name off a newspaper wrapping some chips. (They were the sort who lived on bought chips. But they used to get the chippy to scrape up batter from the bottom of the frier in place of fish.) Anyway, there was an advert for this opera, that was showing in Manchester at the time. It's as well for Aida it was *Aida*. It could have been *Rigoletto* or *Cosi fan Tutte*. Although I don't know; Cosy Boswell would have suited her. She was pretty cosy with an awful lot of men. We've never been entirely sure who Shifty's father was.

We think he was the man Aida lived with before she married Fred. But nothing is certain, you understand. However, thank God, I'm not obliged to write about her. It's her offspring, Shifty, who has somehow managed to wheedle his way into our lives.

Shifty and Celia, torn apart by living...

Shifty! Needless to say this wasn't the name they chose for him, he earned it all by himself. Shifty by nature became Shifty by name. But as I doubt they ever bothered to have him christened, it's as good a name as any other really.

He arrived in our house – or rather Grandad's, because I wasn't going to have him actually sleeping on the premises; we wouldn't have had a stick of furniture by morning – straight from one of Her Majesty's places of confinement. Walton Prison, to be precise. He had just served a six month prison sentence for stealing a Porsche. He drove it all the way from here to London, with the police following but failing to catch him. The reason that they failed was they didn't realise they were chasing a man – or 'a con', to use the vernacular I've been forced to learn since he came into our lives – who was using a rabbit's tactics. Instead of going straight, like a human being, he deviated, like a rabbit. He has been deviating all his life.

It was our Joey who said we should take him in, when he came out of prison, because 'he hadn't got anybody else'.

Well, some people don't have anybody else, because they don't deserve anybody else. Lilo Lil hasn't got anybody else, because she's a TART. Uncle Reggie died alone, with a cup of tea in his hand, because he was too mean to invite anybody else in for a cup. Joey's Roxy hasn't got anybody else, because she wanted everybody else. And Shifty hasn't got anybody else, because everything he *has* got belongs to somebody else. If he so much as puts his hand out it latches onto a belonging that doesn't belong to him.

Grandad, who is usually about as welcoming as British immigration, must have thought he'd died and gone to heaven when Shifty moved in with him. The very first day he got a cashmere pullover, a lot of food, a jigsaw puzzle and a biro – with a new

gold chain for his watch, to follow. Well, of course, he wasn't going to say 'no' was he? They weren't going to put a senior citizen behind bars for receiving stolen goods, were they?

But I have a houseful of young people with time on their hands and dreams in their hearts. Dreams cost money and there's a shortage of cash in this area. Experience has taught me that it only takes one rotten apple to infect a barrel. How else can I explain somebody as straight and honest as Adrian going out and trying to flog stolen video recorders? And involving his little brother Billy in the enterprise? They'd been infected by Shifty, that's how. And of course, being those two they got caught, didn't they? They're now criminals, awaiting trial. They didn't even have the sense to get away with it. But, as I say, I don't blame them; if you put a black shirt into a white wash you end up with a lot of grey sheets. They don't come blacker than Shifty.

Besides, I hate that Irish accent he uses. With good reason. He's like a butch version of Lilo Lil. Not that they come much butcher than her. I sometimes imagine her in her nightgown – always supposing she wears one, the TART. If she does, she'll be all blue ribbons and biceps and z-cup bras.

Joey argued that with Shifty living next door, at least we knew there was somebody with Grandad – and somebody Grandad liked. But would he still like him if he knew the truth; that he was harbouring a felon?

'He hasn't hurt anybody, Mam,' Joey argued.

But of course he's hurt somebody. There are people walking about up to their ears in valium because they were on the motorway the day he took off in that Porsche for London.

He's a bad lot, that's all there is to it. He's the sort, if you opened your gob too wide would steal the gold fillings out of your teeth. And he won't change. He'll always be the same; a buttercup with thorns.

But, of course, I wasn't listened to and, of course, in no time at all I was proved right. He was up to his old, pathetic tricks. He was swapping the sticky tickets on supermarket goods, for example. A jar of coffee for 25 pence? No! The sticky ticket off a biro for 25 pence happened to move over onto his jar of coffee and now there's some poor old dear writing her last Will and Testament with a biro that costs more than her entire estate is worth.

He's like a devious parrot. He sits there, on his perch, watching you. One false move and he'll have your arm off. You won't even notice it's gone until you reach up to switch the light on. And it's no good him pointing out that half the things he steals he wants to give to you for presents. What's the good of that? I'm not going to jail for receiving stolen goods; not on his account.

To cap it all, he keeps claiming that he's only ever made one little indiscretion and that he's being made to pay for it for the rest of his life. But, going for a joy ride in somebody else's Porsche, getting caught and then spending six months in jail is not one little indiscretion. It's a great, big, fully grown crime. It just happens to be the only one, so far, that he's been made to pay for. And what about since he came out? Since he moved in with Grandad? Every time he sets foot out of the door he's liable to bring half a supermarket home. Grandad now has enough food in his cupboard to last him through his after life. He's having a reserve tank fitted to his stomach to cope with the excess. One little indiscretion! Shifty is a fully-fledged hood. He's a convict.

A fully fledged hood

Then there's the 'hanky-panky'. As far as that goes, you'd think he'd invented the art. Not that he's ever stayed long enough with a woman for it to become a fixture of course. Just as they're beginning to think about measuring for wall-to-wall carpet and a new suite, he's off down the motorway in someone else's car, isn't he?

How Celia Higgins thought he was the one for her is a total mystery to me. Well she soon learnt, didn't she? The minute it was beginning to look serious, she couldn't see him for exhaust smoke. But even then she wasn't prepared to give up. That's why she bought No 32. So that she could be living next to him. Her idea was that one day he'd come out of Grandad's on the way to wherever and she'd be scrubbing the step and he'd see her – and very gently . . . she'd frighten him to death; like the rat in the basement – it doesn't do anything in particular, but you know it's there.

'But, what good will that do?' I asked her. 'Where will it get you?'

'Nowhere,' she replied. 'But I'll smile a lot.'

She's clever, Celia is.

Well, of course, where it's got her is, they're back together again in a funny sort of half-on, half-off way. They haven't exactly moved in together. Instead, Celia applied for the job of Grandad's cleaner, and in that way she gets close enough to him to know his every move.

'You only applied for the job so you could harass me,' Shifty told her. 'We were fine without you. I washed, he dried – we had a system.'

'You half-washed and he just rubbed what was left into the cracks,' she said. 'That was your system.'

Celia. You can tell she's intellectual by the book on her chest.

Shifty and Celia, stuck together with glue...

'Well, at least we had peace.'

That's how they carry on. All the time. Why? In the name of 'love'? It's a funny world we live in. So much is done in the name of 'love'. Like, a person'll go and cut down an innocent tree because they 'love the sunlight and the tree was blocking it'. Well, maybe the tree loved the sunlight as well. Did anyone think of that?

'Love' is selfishness in an acceptable form.

Mind, who am I to question the goings-on of other people? Did I do so wonderfully myself that I can tell Shifty and Celia the right and the wrong?

But all I ever wanted was a quiet, respectable life – whatever that might be!

'Listen,' she once told me – Celia, I mean, my friend, Celia Higgins – 'Listen. When I was going out with my first fella, I met the second fella, and shortly after meeting the second fella, I married the first fella, and there I was – a respectable, married lady, with a saucepan in one hand and a cookery book in the other and feeling cheated in my brain. I used to meet the second fella in the afternoons – at The Glade Hotel – and afterwards . . . you know? Afterwards . . . he used to lounge about in a white robe while I was struggling to separate my tights from my knickers and figure out the quickest way home.

'And then at home, with my husband . . . Afterwards again . . . he used to light a cigarette while I used to go downstairs and make him a cup of tea. "How was it for you?" he'd say. "Wonderful," I'd say. "Bloody exhausting," I'd think. The thing is, Nellie, all that energy, all that passion . . . and now what? My ex has run off with a frosty-faced civil servant, fella number two is living with an Amazonian Swede, number three has married a little lady with titled parents and a face like a fruit bat. And me? I'm living next door to the man I love, who steals Porsches and is never there when you want him, and I'm doing his cleaning for him. So what does it all mean? I'll tell you. Life is five minutes long, so grab the laughs. That's what it means.'

DEAR FATHER, HELP ME TO LEARN TO ACCEPT WHAT LIFE CHUCKS AT ME, LIKE MY FRIEND CELIA DOES, AND HELP ME TO FIGHT BACK WITH THE SAME FLAIR AS HER. HELP ME TO FORGIVE SHIFTY IF I MUST. BUT PLEASE DON'T ASK ME TO FORGIVE THE TART WHO HAS TAKEN MY FREDDIE FROM ME AND FROM YOUR ONLY CATHOLIC CHURCH AND CAST HIM INTO OUTER-PROTESTANT-DARKNESS. GIVE ME THE STRENGTH TO WRITE THE NEXT CHAPTER AND REMIND ME TO GRAB THE LAUGHS. AMEN.

Chapter Twelve

Freddie (& Her)

WHEN SOMEBODY LEAVES you for somebody else, it's like being told that how you talk, how you walk, how you eat, how you look, how you ARE, is wrong.

I really don't want this chapter to be the bitter end – but I'm going to find it very hard. It is hard to wake up each morning and have the first thought that enters your head be 'Still no chest. Still no husband.' Because that's what it's all been about. The size of a bosom. That's what's so paralysingly ridiculous. It's always been all down to her rampaging bust, with its devious life of its own. Lilo Lil! She's so big she needed Camell Laird to construct her bra. If she lay flat on the ground for long enough they'd have to re-draw the map of Britain to accommodate two new mountains. And it's this pitiable deformity that's been the cause of everything. All my unhappiness. All the family upsets. All the rows and the fights and the humiliation. All the gossip in the street and the jokes about us. All of this, due to a freak of nature. And, what is worse, it was me that brought this monstrosity into all our lives. It's MY fault. I did it. Wide-eyed and innocent, I opened the door and asked her in.

At the time, Freddie wasn't well. I was running the family. I couldn't do it all – so I decided to get a woman in! To help with the housework. To do some of the odd jobs. Little did I know what her speciality was. I thought she'd do a bit of cleaning; I didn't know she'd tear through the house like a scarlet tornado leaving a wake of destruction behind her and a large gap where my husband once used to be.

Oh, she was such a perfectionist. Everything had to be shining. Everything had to be right. Nothing was too much trouble. She starched Freddie's pillow cases, bleached his sheets, ironed his pyjamas. And then she made up his bed all smooth and professional, just like they do in hospital; even the cover had to be folded just right. Straight and proper, with the hospital corners and the correct amount of sheet showing. I tell you, she created a picture. I could have framed it and sold it at an auction: 'A Matrimonial Bed; by Lilo Lil – a TART'. I suppose the only thing left for her to do after all that exertion was to get in beside him and give his body the same treatment she'd just lavished on his bed.

Freddie Boswell – my husband

That's how it started. I remember he made a most remarkable recovery from his illness; all of a sudden he was smiling again. When I got in one afternoon, there he was sitting up in bed, with a big grin on his face. I should have known at once. He never grinned like that for me. Well, he did. But he hadn't for a while. But I suspected nothing. I trusted him. I made them *both* a cup of tea. That's how much of a fool I am.

Lillian Whittacker. If it hadn't been for her, I sometimes wonder what would have happened to us. Suppose I'd got Mrs Pheelan to come in and look after him? Sixty-five with halitosis? Or that part-time nurse from Westland Street; built like a bean pole with a concave chest?

Suppose he hadn't met Lillian Whittacker – would he have gone out searching until he found her or someone else? Was I so unattractive to him? Was he so . . . bored with me? Or is it just a peculiarity of his that I hadn't come across till then? Does he, in some perverted way, have to suffocate himself every so often between great mountainous cliffs of pink flesh and was my only failing that I couldn't provide him with an adequate venue?

Before her arrival on the scene he'd been like any other ordinary husband; never there when you needed him, pissed when he had to be sober, argumentative to a fault, amorous at inconvenient moments and always hungry.

But he was mine. That's what hurts. He may not have been perfect. We may have spent most nights fighting and making it up. We may sometimes have seemed ridiculous. But I was his – and he was mine.

I have removed the TART from this snap.

I just wish it didn't still hurt so much.

From the minute she came along, nothing was ever the same again. Freddie moved out into a flat – a love nest, I suppose you'd call it. And me? Well, I just tried to carry on as usual, bringing up the family on my own. There was nothing new about that. He'd hardly been a great influence in our lives before. Freddie is a dreamer. He sees colours where I see black and white. The small print is always in black and white.

If there was any change for me after he moved out it was probably that I started going more regularly to confession. It wasn't only that I needed the comfort of faith; I wanted somebody to talk to, to tell my troubles to, to share my hopes and fears. I couldn't burden our Joey with all that and there's no better listener than the Almighty – though you don't always know what he's thinking.

Father Dooley told me that I had to learn forgiveness. Father Dooley says that there is nothing that cannot be forgiven. But Father Dooley changed his tune the day I told him Freddie had turned Protestant. Apparently the good Lord can stand anything, so long as you're a Catholic. We are not expected to forgive him for going over to the other side. It's a relief really. I feel as though God has found out what a two-timing snake Freddie Boswell really is. Up until then, I had an uncomfortable feeling that he thought it was all my fault.

After the docks closed down, Freddie was out of work. That didn't help, of course. But then most of his mates were in the same state and Freddie had never treated dock work as a vocation, if you know what I mean. So it wasn't a blow to him not having to live his life by the hooter. Not that he wanted to be idle; he needed something to get him out of the house each day. But as long as I was there, putting food on the table, he was in no hurry to find alternative employment.

But then once he left home things altered dramatically. He had to start fending for himself. He had a flat of his own to maintain for a start and then he discovered that food didn't arrive in a magical way on the table. It had to be bought and paid for. So he went out and he got himself a job with the council. I could have called him a council worker, but the precise nature of his job belied that grand title. He pushed a muck cart round the streets, sweeping up litter. This is so typical of him, somehow. Wandering along in a daze, dreaming in Technicolor, without a thought for how he looked or what people thought of him. A street sweeper. That's what he was. And – d'you know? He claimed he'd never been happier. Whether this bliss was due to pushing a little yellow cart about or to his extra-marital arrangements it is not for me to say.

Meanwhile all the children were missing him. Funny about kids. You bring them into the world, you fight for their survival, you wheel, deal and swindle to keep them clothed and fed and what happens? They end up having ideas of their own. Each one of them, like a Judas, creeping off to see him. Each one of them putting in a plea for me to have him back.

Have him back! There was a time I thought they were suggesting that the TART should move in as well.

'Oh Mam,' they'd say, 'we love him, Mam. He's our dad and we love him.'

That word again! 'Love'. I suppose he thought he 'loved' her as well.

She once sent me a letter. The nerve of the woman – sending ME a letter. She runs away with my husband and then she has the nerve to write to me. 'Could we have a chat?' she wrote. The impudent, presumptuous, contemptuous COW.

Well, she'd met her match with me. I'm not one of those women who lies in bed wondering what to do. I knew what to do. I'm not the type to put up with anything for the sake of peace, or keep my mouth shut for the sake of peace, or wait for everything to blow over for the sake of peace. I knew exactly how to solve the problem and get all the peace I wanted. Kill the pair of them; that's what I should have done.

'Per'aps you will understand me better when we've talked,' she wrote. The COW. What is there to understand about a TART?

Next thing I knew, she turned up on the doorstep. My own front doorstep, with a TART standing on it. Worse than that – the FAMILY TART. I have rarely been so humiliated.

'I want to talk,' she says, 'that's all.'

The picture of happiness, with his muck cart

That was ALL? Well, of course it was all. She'd done everything else that was possible. Talking was all that was left.

'We're both intelligent people,' she says.

Intelligent? Her? Any brains she's ever had had migrated to her knickers long since.

'Get off my doorstep,' I told her and I gave her a shove.

'I warn you,' she says, 'people don't push me around.'

Oh, don't they?! There was no holding me then. I could not wait to get at her.

Look, I'm not proud of it, I know that I am cursed with a terrible temper. But, dear Father, I was provoked that day.

'At least I know how to keep a man happy,' she yells – for all the street to hear.

'You're scum, that's what you are. Scum!' I told her.

Grandad had to separate us. An old man, veteran of two world wars, with a hearing aid and an incontinence grant, forced out into the street to separate two grown women before they killed each other. That's what she'd brought me to. Fighting, in my own street, like an alley cat. It was a day of shame.

I had to ask her in. We couldn't continue shouting on the doorstep with all the neighbours listening and taking notes.

'I just wanted to explain,' she said.

'You took my husband.'

'I didn't take him,' she said. 'You can't take people.'

But she did, no matter what she says. She seduced him with her red hair and her red fingernails and her marauding chest.

'You used to walk down this street past this house, with all your assets on red alert,' I told her.

'I did used to live in this street,' she said. 'I had to walk past to get to my house. What did you expect me to do,' she said. 'Take up hang gliding.'

And then she had the nerve to say:

'I want to settle down. I want to have a permanent relationship. If you don't want Freddie . . .'

She had the cheek to stand there, calling my Freddie, Freddie. The familiar cow!

'. . . if you don't want him anymore, then I know I can work at it,' she said. 'But if you do want him, then I'm old enough and wise enough to know that I can't win. Oh, for a while, perhaps. But roots go deep, leaves sprout . . .'

'I see,' I said, 'so first you take him, then, when he's worn out three years later, you come and ask if I'll take him back. People do that with hire-purchase televisions . . .'

I was shaken, I don't mind saying.

'Not if you want him back,' she said. 'For God's sake, don't you understand?'

'No, I do not understand,' I told her. 'We come from different planets, you and me. TART,' I yelled.

'Don't ever call me that again,' she said.

'Don't ever come near this house again,' I said. 'Tart,' I said. 'Tart.'

But you can't keep that sort of anger up for too long. It wears you out. Then where are you? Left, looking at each other, not knowing how best to finish it.

'Look,' she said, 'we're both woman. We have handbags and ovaries. We're as devious and as clever as a gifted monkey – and here we are fighting over a little man who pushes a yellow cart . . .'

Grandad to the rescue. This snap was taken by Mrs Porter at No.53. Joey had to buy the negatives off her.

'Is that how you see him?' I said.

'No,' she replied. 'It's how I thought you might see him.'

And I heard myself saying:

'He's a secretive, perceptive, poetic man. He's a free, wandering soul. He brushes the streets because he needs his mind to dream with. He needs both of us, now and then, and maybe he wants neither of us permanently . . .'

Sometimes you say something and you know as you're saying it, that the words will lodge for ever in your memory; because they're the truth. It was the truth and we both knew it.

She put her elbows on the table, where half an hour before I'd been leading an ordinary life, baking and minding my own business. She put her head in her hands and gave a long sigh. I thought she was settling in for the duration.

'Now get your Irish elbows off my table and out of my life and my cheese flaps,' I told her. 'Go on, out of my house and on your way.'

I have no love for that woman, no respect, no compassion. She showed me up and I will never forgive her for that. I always had my pride and my dignity; I always kept our private life secret from the neighbours. But that day, she stamped into my world and made me reveal everything – my anger, my private sorrow, my temper, my marital problems, my knickers even – to the entire street.

I mean, you'd lose respect for the Queen if she came charging out of the Palace and beat somebody up in the Mall, wouldn't you?

And all for what? What good did it do? None. I might just as well not have bothered.

You can't hurt Lilo Lil – you can't get past her chest for a start. When I think of Freddie rummaging his way through that lot it makes me despair for the human race. Why is it so special for him? Why? I've asked myself the question so many times over the years, but I never get an adequate answer.

I suppose, in a way, it's a sort of addiction; like smoking or alcohol or drugs. He's got a breast addiction. Her brassiere should carry a government health warning. But, if that's the case, what possessed him to marry me? I mean if he wanted gargantuan boobs he only had to look at me to know I wasn't the one for him. And he did more than look, down at The Grafton of a Saturday night, when we were both young and he thought the sun rose and set specially for me.

I suppose the fact is you don't have to marry a publican in order to be a dipso-maniac. Maybe he wanted a nice ordinary chest beside him most of the time and a quick sortie into Disney World once in a while. Then the craving got the better of him and he started wanting it all the time. One thing is certain, he doesn't seem to be able to do without her for very long. Just when I think the coast's clear, when I think he's come to his senses and ditched her; a little warning light flashes on in my head – and I know he's got her hidden somewhere, lurking, ready to pounce. If only I could accept that. Why don't I go around expecting the worst? Then at least I'd be prepared. Why does it always have to come as a shock?

He was in a terrible accident once. A lorry mowed into a watchman's hut while he was sheltering inside. We all rushed down, worried sick. I thought the end had come. I thought I'd lost him. I knew if I had, my heart would never mend. I mean, he may be a pain in the arse, but I wouldn't want him dead. But no, they managed to dig him out . . . and while we were basking in the relief and offering prayers of gratitude to God that he'd only got a broken leg, they were going on digging, weren't they? And they went and dug her out as well. Lilo Lil! I swear she'll pop out of his coffin at his funeral, just to spite me. I mean, what were they doing together in the hut in the first place? When it hadn't even been raining. No, I don't think I want to know, somehow.

It hurts every time. It hurts, Freddie.

They finally dismissed him from the cleansing department. I suppose his dreaming got in the way of his work. And that night, he walked off with his muck cart. He just couldn't do without it. He felt naked without something in front of him to push. I wouldn't mind, but where was he when there were prams to push?

So, he was arrested for stealing a muck cart. He was put into jail for stealing a MUCK CART.

I sometimes think I'm going mad.

We all had to put on out best clothes and go to his trial. Why couldn't he have been a bank robber or have masterminded an international fraud syndicate? Why couldn't he have hacked computers? Something half-way respectable. Why did he have to be emblazoned across the *Echo* and the *Post* for having nicked a MUCK CART?

Freddie outside the court house – not a care in the world

Why?

Why do these things happen to me? I'm a God-fearing woman. He turned up at the church for our wedding looking like a burst pillow. He turned up at the hospital when I had our first, drunk beyond repair. He runs off with an Irish TART. Then he's a thief.

I began to think there was only murder left.

Oh well, of course, we all went to his trial, didn't we? Of course we did; the united family again. With the exception of our Billy that is, who somehow seemed to think it was more important to go and get married in a registry office instead – thereby not only not standing by his father in his hour of need, but also denying me the right to be at my own son's nuptials. But that's another story and besides, I've already told it.

And, at the trial, what happens? The toffee-nosed magistrate announces for all the world to hear that Mr Boswell is living apart from his wife and family with a Miss Lillian Whittacker, known locally as . . .

'Don't you dare utter Lilo Lil's name in this court,' I yelled. 'This is our private, secret, intimate life and she is a TART.'

But we have no private life, do we? Not any more. You've seen to that, Freddie.

Even when I had him back living in the house, sleeping on the sofa in the front room, even then, he was creeping off to see her. It's a drug. It's the only way I can explain it.

And now we have to be very careful, because all of a sudden he's a sick man. He's coronary material. He's got a heart condition.

A heart condition! I ask you. Wouldn't it be the heart, with Freddie Boswell? He couldn't have in-growing toenails or pernicious anaemia, could he? No. Not him.

He mustn't get over excited now or push a cart up steep hills. He has to rest a lot. I have to watch his diet.

I don't want him to die. Oh God, I don't want him to die.

Celia Higgins reckons he'll outlive us all. We're so worried for him, we treat him like a bit of china.

'You don't slam a door with one hinge,' she said.

True, but I still get close to it. I have this awful temper and the one person who is guaranteed to make me lose it is him.

He went and got another job. Hot Dog Vendor! He's like one of those continuous tapes of music they play in lifts. If you go up and down long enough the repetition will drive you insane. Hot Dog Vendor? I could say he works in the fast food trade. But the fact is that now, instead of ambling round the streets pushing a muck cart he's ambling round the streets pushing a cart selling the muck that used to go into his muck cart. If anything it's a retrograde step. But I can't say too much, because of his heart.

But I'd like to do a deal with him, for all that. I'd like to say to him, 'You push whatever cart you like, love, only give up that TART. You come upstairs to your own bed, where you belong, instead of sleeping on the sofa which isn't really long enough, but first give up that TART. We'll be a happy family, love, united and strong. Only, please, PLEASE give her up, Freddie, before she suffocates you or she puts that extra strain on your heart and it's too late.'

But, of course, I say nothing of the sort. I'm not given to making speeches. Not like her. At our Aveline's wedding, when she arrived – pushing herself in on our side of the

The TART at our Aveline's wedding.
Adrian's expression speaks for us all.

Freddie – my husband

aisle as though she was family – she made a fine speech then . . . she could have ruined the service.

'This'll never happen to me,' she said, 'a wedding. I spent all my life looking for the right man, and he turned out to be yours.'

Then why doesn't she leave us alone, I thought. She must know how hopeless men are. If you don't want them eating the cakes, remove the tin.

'I could have kept quiet, of course,' she said, 'I could have been deceitful and artful and never said a word. That's what most people do, you know, never say a word, but I was honest with you. I fought a losing battle, but I fought it out in the open. Now all I want to do is see him standing there with his daughter. I want a picture to keep in my mind's eye when I go. Oh, yes, I'm going,' she said. 'There comes a time when there's nothing left to do, but go.'

Well then, go, I thought. I'm sorry, but I got in first – so go. And the story is that she has – back to Ireland. But why is it, I wonder, that that little warning light keeps flashing?

Partly because, well, it's a bit like Dr Who and the Daleks. Every time he thinks he's wiped them out there's some little cog that rolls over to another little cog and you know that there's one little Dalek going back on the delivery line. I've thought she's gone so often; it's just like that. But I've grown to know that, after I've turned my back, each time a little bit of chest in the heap on the floor begins to wobble and then to pulse – denoting there's life still in there, preparing to pounce once more.

Partly, of course, it's on account of the fact that I don't know what goes on in Freddie's head. But I sometimes see a distant look come into his eyes and he has a dreamy sort of a grin on his face and I know he's thinking of her.

And that hurts as much as anything else.

DEAR FATHER, HELP ME NOT TO WANT TO MURDER LILO LIL AND PLEASE DON'T LET FREDDIE DIE. I KNOW I'VE BEEN A JEALOUS WOMAN, FATHER. I KNOW I'VE RANTED AND RAVED AND NOT BEHAVED AT MY BEST ALWAYS. BUT I LOVE HIM, FATHER – WHATEVER THAT WORD MEANS – AND WHAT IS MORE, HE DOES ME, THE STUPID IDIOT; IT'S JUST THAT HE GETS CONFUSED BY ALL THAT FLESH. BLESS THE LITTLE ANI-MALS, FATHER. THEY SOMEHOW MANAGE NOT TO LET 'HANKY-PANKY' GET IN THE WAY OF LIVING. THAT'S A RARE GIFT, THAT IS. ONE WE COULD ALL DO WITH. AMEN.

The Roman Holiday

I THOUGHT I should include some snaps from our holiday in Rome. We went as a united family – but I daresay we all had a little dream of our own. Anyway, I'll let the pictures speak for themselves.

Celia and Shifty doing the town

SHOPPING LIST

Suntan oil

Sun screen

Water purifier for Grandad

Mosquito spray, net,
  anything that works

Toilet rolls

Elasto

Corn

Tea-b

Corn

Italia

Indig

New

The Trevi Fountain – I know what I was wishing for

The nearest I got to the Holy Father - his bodyguard

Even a Proddy vicar catches the Latin romance...

Julie and Billy - they would pose where the gladiators used to kill themselves, wouldn't they?

Grandad remembers – hormones and adrenaline

Sightseeing in style. Me, clutching handbag for fear of theft

The English abroad. The last day

Chapter Thirteen

WOULDN'T IT TURN out that I would end up with chapter thirteen – an unlucky number? But I suppose I must say something about myself, even if most things have already been said.

I am a woman of uncertain age. (I can't even always remember it myself.) I have five kids, one aged father, a mongrel dog without his bits and pieces and a husband who is hanging onto his only by my good will.

I help my hair colour when I'm in the mood. Well, why not enhance what nature gave you?

I'm a reasonable cook; or at least I'm quick. I provide variety and I serve healthy, nourishing fare for carnivores, vegetarians and assorted pets.

I am a God-fearing woman, who goes to mass regularly and never misses a chance to confess. Furthermore, our priest, Father Dooley, always gets a welcome in our house and never goes away empty handed.

I have tried, through these pages, to give some picture of what life is like for a Scouse Lady in the 1980s. If or when my family read this, they will, no doubt, be surprised by much of what I have to say, shocked at how much I know and disappointed that I have left so much out. To them I can only say: don't worry. Knowing what I know has never – quite – stopped me caring about you all: I'm beyond shocking; and there isn't a book big enough to contain everything that has happened to us.

But then I ask myself, have I come clean about ME?

Would I have wanted things to be different?

Sometimes I've thought so – but things never work out how you imagine.

Like, I was recently sitting on a park bench, surrounded by shopping bags, having a quiet moment. The trouble with a big family is you never seem to get any time to yourself. I need that, sometimes; I expect we all do. So, there I was, sitting feeding the birds with fresh bread and for once in my life not rushing home to cook another meal for the menagerie until I was good and ready, when a fella walking his dog stopped and said 'Good morning'.

Just that. 'Good morning.'

Is that how it always starts? I wouldn't know. Not that anything really 'started', you understand – he was just a nice, straightforward fella, with a dog, out for a stroll – but it could have.

His name was Derek. He had a kind face. Well, maybe I thought 'why not?' My husband was off romping on Lilo Lil. My children were each in their own way exploring life's highways and byways like bloodhounds on the scent. My father was safely tucked up with a good breakfast under his belt. Even our dog was happily lying back, remembering past conquests. (Since his operation, he sleeps with a permanent smile on his face and his tail keeps wagging.) And me? I suppose I just felt . . . high and dry; on the shelf; past my sell-by date. So, why shouldn't I think, 'why not?'

Well, of course, it's me I'm talking about, isn't it? That's the answer to 'why not?' So, nothing really happened between Derek and me. We went out a few times; had champagne on the deck of a cabin cruiser, walks in the park, drives in the country – nothing common, you understand. He was in every way a gentleman. He drove me home, more than once we were 'seen' in the street. But, I'm afraid we couldn't have measured up to the gossip . . . because of me.

Once he asked to kiss me. But I explained that I wasn't very keen on being kissed. I said kissing was for other people – like sometimes you wear something and it's not right for you: a short skirt, for instance. I'd feel as silly being kissed, I told him, as wearing a short skirt.

Why am I telling you this?

It's the might-have-beens. The others all have their stories – well, so do I, I'm trying to say.

In the end I did let Derek kiss me – just once, while we were saying goodbye. It's hardly the stuff of grand passion this, is it? But, you see, it wasn't for me, all that deceit, all that affair stuff. I have to be straight. It's the way I am. I couldn't tell lies. I tried, but it didn't work somehow. But no more could I tell the family that they'd have to get their own dinners today because I'm off out to have an affair. Could I? Not me. Not my family.

When we were in Rome last year, I found myself going off the beaten track one day. I was on my own, and I knew just where I was heading. You see once, years ago, when I was younger, a man – an Italian man no less – presented me with a rose in a little alleyway and he told me that I was 'Bella! Bella!' and that he would 'wait for ever for me'. Well, you always remember something like that – or at least, I do, because it hasn't happened very often. So, I thought, 'Go back, Nellie – back to the scene of your romantic encounter. Live the dream. Feel young again. Believe you're Bella! Bella!' Well, the alley was there! I could hear a lot of Italian shouting coming from one of the houses – funny how a domestic tiff is recognisable no matter what language is used. And then, as I was standing there, half in the past, a window flew open and a middle-aged, overweight, spaghetti-gutted man – who could just have been my beautiful Gigolo of yesteryear – leaned out . . . and tipped a bowl of dishwater straight over my head!

That, if you ask me, is life! Like my friend Celia said – 'you've just got to grab the laughs'!

Me

So – no dreams for me, thanks. I'll just take what comes.

Our Jack is coming home. There could be no better news than that. The first of my children to actually strike it rich. I can't wait to see him. He's done so well over in America, selling food to the gay community that I think they should be given their own saint.

Our Adrian is something of a local hero, having behaved in a way that I find almost unbelievable for him. Apparently he, single-handed, tackled a mugger who was running off with an old lady's handbag. She was so grateful to him, she sent him a cheque for £200. The media has got hold of the story. It's all photographs and interviews. He's just now been on local radio again. Every time he tells the story it sounds more exciting, more bloodthirsty and far less likely, somehow. Of course, we must never forget that Adrian is a creative artist.

Our Billy – poor soul; well, what can I say? The sooner his divorce is over and done with the sooner he can start living again. I mean he's still only a baby; he's got plenty of time to make some sense out of his life. He just happens to be the only baby who has already fathered a child, been married, played the mouth organ and cymbals at the same time (more or less) in public and run a sandwich round. He's packed a life-time into a moment. But then he raced through puberty as though there was a prize for coming in first and I swear he was born with a full set of dentures in his gob, so I don't know why I should be surprised.

Aveline is a problem – but then girls are, aren't they? Six months married, and there's still no sign of a pregnancy. We took her to the doctor – but of course he only confirmed what I already knew; there is no reason why she shouldn't be repopulating the entire universe. On her side, that is. Well, of course I knew that. She comes from strong stock. But what about him? What about the Reverend Oswald Carter? The doctor suggested he should go in for a sperm count. Well, I wasn't surprised. You've only got to look at Oswald to see he's spermless.

Our Joey is worrying me just at the moment. He's keeping something from me and I have a feeling it's something I'm not going to like. He had a letter from Her Majesty's Collector of Taxes, not long since – and letters from that office don't usually put a smile on your face. But I must say I'm puzzled; we make a point of not involving ourselves with taxation. We are scrupulous about that. We don't want to cost the government money doing our books. It'll come out sooner or later, I know. But Joey has been and still is my right hand, my mainstay, the head of the family, and if there's something worrying him – then it's bound to worry me.

Me again

A happy day on the river.
But I wish Freddie had been there.

And Freddie? Well, he's got himself an allotment now. He claims he's always wanted to grow things – but I think it's just an excuse for him to get a wheelbarrow and to have something in front of him to push. He still gets that distant look from time to time and a grin on his face that makes me uncomfortable – but Lilo Lil *is* supposed to be in Ireland, and you can usually tell if she's back in town; the locals board up their windows and the lingerie shops put their staff on overtime. He's got a hut on his allotment and he goes down there to dream. One thing you can't do is share a person's dreams. So I don't go down. What'd I want to be sitting in a hut on an allotment, having a lot of gardeners leaning on their spades gawping at me? But that distant look puzzles me. I don't want to see the little warning light flashing . . .

So, this chapter is supposed to be about me, isn't it? And here am I writing more about them again.

Well, that's how it is, you see. All that . . . all this book . . . it is me. I am my family. I daresay Germaine Greer would have a fit to hear me, but I can't help it. I've had years of training for the part. Wife and mother, that's me. If I tried to be anything else, I'd only get it wrong. I've spent a lifetime in this street, and over half of it with a family to feed and see to. So is it any wonder it's the only part I know how to play?

Mrs Nellie Boswell, 30 Kelsall Street.

With five kids, an aged father, several hangers-on, a mongrel dog and a straying husband.

A united group . . . some of the time. A pack of scoundrels . . . once in a while. My family.

'Us & Ours.'

But where am I?

I sometimes look in the mirror and I wonder who I really am – me – who am I?

DEAR FATHER, BLESS MY FAMILY, WITH ALL THEIR WEAKNESSES AND LITTLE QUIRKS. PRESERVE AND KEEP THEM FROM EVIL. AND BLESS ALL THE LITTLE ANIMALS, WHO MAKE MORE SENSE TO ME AS EVERY DAY PASSES. DON'T LET MAN GO ON HURTING THEM, FATHER. FOR EVERY TIME A SPARROW FALLS TO A NASTY CHILD'S AIR PISTOL OR A WHALE DISAPPEARS FROM THE DEEP; EVERY TIME A FOX IS HUNTED TO DEATH OR A BADGER IS GOADED FOR VILE SPORT; EVERY TIME A CHICKEN IS KEPT IN A STINKING BATTERY HOUSE OR A COW IS PERSECUTED FOR PROFIT; EVERY TIME, FATHER, ALL MEN ARE DIMINISHED. PROTECT US, DEAR FATHER, FROM BECOMING THE VILE BRUTES OF THE EARTH. AND FINALLY, FATHER, GRANT ME ONE LAST REQUEST, IF IT'S RIGHT FOR ME TO HAVE IT. PLEASE DON'T LET THE LITTLE WARNING LIGHT THAT I SEE FLASHING BE TELLING ME THE TRUTH. DEAR FATHER, DON'T LET LILO LIL SHOW UP AGAIN, BECAUSE, IF SHE DOES, I FEAR FOR MY OWN SOUL. I'LL STRIKE FIRST AND THINK AFTER. FORGIVE ME IN ADVANCE, FATHER, BUT I'LL SKIN HER ALIVE IF SHE SHOWS UP HERE AGAIN. I KNOW IT'S WRONG. I KNOW, FATHER. BUT IT'S A HEAVY CROSS YOU ASK ME TO BEAR – A VERY HEAVY CROSS – AND I AM A WOMAN WITH A TERRIBLE TEMPER. AMEN.